A Light Shining in Cornwall

By
Josephine Cunnington Edwards

TEACH Services, Inc.
P U B L I S H I N G
www.TEACHServices.com • (800) 367-1844

Copyright © 2019 TEACH Services, Inc.
ISBN-13: 978-1-57258-325-2 (Paperback)
Library of Congress Control Number: 2006920049

Published by

Dedicated to
Laura and Frank Arnett

Billy Bray 1794–1868

FOREWORD

My father often regaled our family with stories of Billy Bray, the Cornish evangelist whose name was a household word among the Bible Christian Methodists of southwest England during the middle years of the nineteenth century. Thus with a delightful sense of recall, I read this account of Bray by Mrs. Edwards. It has caught the fervor and naivete' of this incomparable representative of the Bryanite religious revival movement.

My recollections of the Lanner Bible Christian Chapel, which I attended as a small boy, are vivid, especially of the protracted meetings which rated the merit of conversions according to the noisy demonstrations they provoked. I remember instances where attendants shouting "Praise the Lord" and "Hallelujah" carried converts, overcome to the point of fainting and exhaustion, to their homes on stretchers.

It was in this religious milieu that Billy Bray flourished. Aggressive, eccentric, untutored, yet possessing a singular grace and charm, he was unpredictable in both his pulpit utterances and methods of labor. Christ and Satan were real entities to him, and his audible conversations with them took on the spirit of fellowship with one and of challenge to the other.

A LIGHT SHINING IN CORNWALL

Although a representative of the lay or local preacher plan of the Methodist Church, as a Bryanite Billy Bray was a free-lance preacher, exhorting when he would and building chapels where be could. Most of these places of worship were exploits in faith, and prayer on an "ask and receive" basis never had a greater witness than in this exponent of an uncomplicated gospel. Whenever be preached, even standing room was at a premium, and on occasion as many would be listening through the open windows of the chapel as were seated in the sanctuary. He often irritated the Established churchmen and formal religionists of his day, but in face-to-face contention with them, his radiant countenance and unashamed zeal conciliated the most obtrusive.

Generous beyond the call of duty, Billy sometimes gave away his wages as a miner to the needy and indigent, arriving at home with empty pockets on payday to his patient family, whom he adjured with happy confidence that "the Lord will provide." And contrary to the predictions of the most skeptical, the Lord whom Billy Bray served always did.

The obscurities of the old Cornish idiom have prevented the author from fully using the vernacular, which to natives of that romantic promontory of the British Isles has nostalgic overtones. The dialogue, however, here and there retains some of the expressions still current among the populace. The total impact of the book is the impression of a deeply dedicated, though quixotic and quaint, personality.

H. M. TIPPETT, M.A., Litt.D.

CHAPTER ONE

NEARLY four centuries after the arrival of the English on the islands of Britain, they realized that they must subdue the wild inhabitants of a narrow, tapering peninsula thrusting westward into the restless Atlantic. This was no easy task, for the Celts of Cornwall were warriors of dash and fire. From this strange country jutting wedge-shaped out into the cold ocean we have inherited legends of King Arthur and his Knights of the Round Table. Some of the names from these fanciful stories ring in our ears, names like Tintagel, Camelford, and Dozemore Pool.

An amusing legend says that the devil never ventured to cross the River Tamar from England into the duchy of Cornwall because he was afraid someone would catch him and put him into a Cornish pasty. The Tamar River divides Devonshire and Cornwall, and Cornish men actually feel they are leaving England when they go into Cornwall.

Even so, Cornwall has been closely linked with England since the fourteenth century, for the Black Prince was called the Duke of Cornwall, a title still held by the English king's oldest son, who is also called the Prince of Wales. Cornwall has interesting ruins and relics all over its rocky peninsula. Stone circles, massive dolmens, windswept barrows, cliff castles, and remains of villages at least three or four thousand years old dot the landscape. Among the sand dunes of Perranporth is a little Celtic church that is fifteen hundred years old. It is called the oratory of St. Piran. Piranus is the patron saint of the Cornish miners. In Cornwall the Christian religion has been practiced from Roman times. This is better than England can boast of, for barbarians lived in England at the time the Cornish were worshiping God.

In the middle of Cornwall, near the ancient city of Truro, lies a small village named Twelveheads. Here on the first of June, 1794, a baby boy named Billy Bray was born. He was to become famous throughout England for his service to the King of the universe.

Twelveheads was just a tiny hamlet of only a few thatched cottages, homes of tinsmiths and miners. In the center of the village stood a Methodist chapel, built when John Wesley and John Nelson came to Cornwall and started that denomination.

Billy Bray's grandfather became a Methodist during those terrible times of persecution. Mobs often gathered with knives and stones when dissenting Christians met to worship. It was dangerous to worship differently in those days. People were strongly prejudiced against "sects," as they called the new churches.

When Billy was small, his father, a good man, died; so the boy went to live with his pious

Methodist grandfather. Of course he went to church regularly while growing up, but only because he had to. He longed to be free of all this "religious foolishness," to do things he could not do under his grandfather's eagle eye. Often he looked at his grandfather's kind old face and rebelled against the man's goodness. He thought of all the exciting things he would try out if he could just leave home. It did not occur to him that the tea, bread, and good pasty he freely ate would be hard to get if he were on his own.

At last, at the age of seventeen, Billy left. joyously, hurriedly, he went over into Devonshire to find work. "Now I'm going to have one good time," he thought, "better than I've ever seen or known in the world." Although he missed the regular meals, the warm bed, and protection, be stubbornly determined to wring a wild good time out of life.

Once settled in his new location, he chose his companions, the worst scum around Tavistock, you can be sure. All of his grandfather's teaching seemed to be instantly forgotten. Billy and his chums wasted their money at the pubs (public houses) and thought themselves happy when roaring drunk. They wore ragged clothes, for they didn't spend their hard-earned pence for good things. They never thought of tomorrow, or of God, or of anything but themselves.

One night Billy and one of his companions drank themselves dead drunk in the pretty town of Tavistock. They reeled out into the night and headed toward their poor home. Out of town, heading toward the bleak, barren moor, fumbling and stumbling along narrow lanes, they ran onto a large horse also wandering there.

"A horse! A horse!" shouted Billy incredulously, feeling the animal all over. "Why not ride 'im? My legs feel wobbly like boiled dumplin'. We'll get home sooner and easier if we ride 'im!"

The two boys, drunk and foolish, managed to climb onto the willing old horse's back. Away they galloped, bouncing toward their dreary dwelling, to their rough straw pallets to sleep off their intoxication. But the horse had no good guides. The night being dark and the lane narrow, he soon stumbled and fell heavily, nearly mashing and killing both boys.

After much suffering and pain, Billy recovered, but he had not learned his lesson. As soon as he was well, he started right in again.

One night he fought another drunk for some silly reason he couldn't even remember later. They pawed and poked and bit and scratched, reeling all over the rough taproom in their efforts to injure one another. In the fracas Billy's hat fell into the fireplace and burned. Now what would he do? He had no money to buy another. The alehouse keeper got most of his money. In those days all boys and men wore hats. It was a necessity, since the wind from the Atlantic blew across Tavistock, and the bleak cold of the moors penetrated to one's bones.

Billy didn't care what he did (the commandments meant not a thing to him), so he grabbed a hat—someone else's—put it on his head, and staggered off to his miserable lodging.

Soon awakened by a loud knocking, he heard the owner of the hat outside the door in conversation with the parish peace officer. Billy narrowly escaped jail over that incident. He had to do without ale for several days in order to buy himself a hat.

In later years Billy could never recall those times without deep shame and sorrow. Again and again in his wickedness he escaped almost certain death.

One time he was working in an underground mine when he heard a "scat" (cracking noise) overhead. As he ran out, about forty tons of rubble fell down where he had been working just a minute before.

CHAPTER TWO

BAD LUCK continued to dog Billy's footsteps. He was fired from his job at Tavistock because of insolence to his boss. Miserable as his lot had been, he was in even sorrier straits; now he knew real need. Drifting away from Tavistock to another part of Devonshire, he actually went to live in a beer shop. Lying on a miserable pallet under the counter, he dropped off to troubled sleep amid cursing, vulgar talk, and the sour smell of beer. Probably he did the dirty, menial tasks around the tavern in return for his miserable lodging. Yet even in that dark hour, God saw Billy Bray and longed to save him.

Poorer and more ragged than when he left, Billy finally wandered back to Twelveheads, seven years later. He returned, not a silly boy looking forward to freedom, but a drunkard with a sick head and a sicker stomach. He was far from the freedom he had gone to find. Instead, a thousand chains of habit bound him, a bondage of body and spirit from which be could not free himself.

Now he had a home of sorts, but it was definitely not a happy one. He had married a country girl named Joey. She knew hunger, cold, and nakedness, and bore it with patience. Again and again she would leave her babies in their wretched home and go search for her husband. She always knew where to go. Where else would he be but at beer shops, spending money she and the babies needed for food, coal, and clothing? Neither Joey nor Billy knew any happiness in those days, nothing but drunkenness for Billy and privation and suffering for his little family.

One winter night, with the fuel gone and the house freezing cold, Billy went out to get some coal. On the way home he stopped at a beer shop and stayed until drunk. Joey, having gone out to hunt for him, found her coal in front of the tavern and Billy riotously drunk inside. Patiently she wheeled the coal home, knowing full well that Billy loved neither her nor the children as well as his beer.

CHAPTER THREE

SOMEHOW, from somewhere, a book by John Bunyan, *Visions of Heaven and Hell*, came into Billy's possession.

One evening be was reading the book, inwardly trembling at what he read. Inside him a little voice urged him to go get a drink and forget his conscience. Horrible fear crushed his soul. He knew he had done nothing but evil all his life. He knew he was headed for destruction, and unless he reformed, he was doomed forever.

He began to read the remarkable book in November, 1823. A strong desire to be a better man slowly began to grow in his heart.

Working at her humble tasks while Billy sat absorbed in the book, Joey remarked, "It's a wonderful thing to be right with God. I remember so well the time of my conversion. It was so sweet, yet bitter, too. I can't begin to tell you what a person enjoys who serves the Lord."

Billy looked up at her face. "Why don't you begin again, Joey?" he asked her gently.

She looked at him in surprise. This was not like Billy. He was usually swaggering, bragging, drunk. This was a humble Billy, thinking thoughts she did not dream him capable of.

I might begin if you did," he added, a wistful look on his face.

Joey wondered. A light seemed to break in the darkness of her world. Could it be? Could there ever be some joy in her life?

That evening was different from most evenings—Billy didn't go to the alehouse. joyously, yet fearfully, Joey performed the last duties before they went to bed. Would it last? This was a Billy she could love. The other Billy—drunken, cruel, and lazy—she dreaded. Life with him was as hopeless as trying to mop up the sea. Only the thought of her children, of working for them, sustained her; and even so, it was terrible to see them going about ragged and hungry.

Billy lay in bed listening to the even breathing of his wife, the soft sighs of his little ones on their rough pallets across the room. He reviewed his life, groaning miserably as he realized his failure as a husband and father. The devil had had a strong hold on Billy Bray. Suddenly a great desire to be converted, to have his life changed completely, flooded him.

"If Joey would get converted first," he muttered to himself. "If only she would, then she could show me how to be saved." She had not been such a degenerate sinner as he, and she could soon be forgiven, be reasoned. It might take a long time for him. He lay there, growing more tense and tortured as the moments passed.

By three o'clock in the morning be writhed in such agony that he could not bear it any longer. Leaping out of bed, he dropped to his knees for the first time in his life. In that first encounter with God, he talked as he was to talk to Him, friend to Friend, the rest of his life. The more he prayed, the more he felt like praying.

CHAPTER FOUR

THE FIRST working day of the new year was known as "setting day." Miners, farmers, and others made new work contracts then. To celebrate, they had the habit of stopping by the alehouse to eat and drink. Naturally the lot of them got drunk, Billy usually the worst. When he started cursing, his blasphemies became so fearful that one man said, "Billy's oaths must come from hell, for they smell of sulphur!"

Billy, a marvelous entertainer, kept the boys in such a state of hilarity that he was very popular. His favorite sport was to ridicule sacred things.

But when setting day came that year, to the amazement of his companions, Billy did not join in the fun-making as he had always done before. He was strangely quiet now. Naturally his companions noticed the change. One of them swore angrily at him.

Billy turned his serious eyes upon his former crony. "You must give an account of that someday," he said quietly.

Angered even more, his companion answered mockingly, "Shall we all go to the Bryanites meeting?" ("Bryanites," the local term for the Bible Christians, came from the name of their founder, William O' Bryan. The Bible Christians resulted from an offshoot of the Wesleyan Methodist Church.)

"Better go there than go to hell," Billy replied.

The conversation became heated then, with Billy taking the side of Christianity as loudly as be used to deride it.

"Hey, Billy, talk softer! You're too noisy, roaring at us that way. After all, you used to be with us, remember?" a red-faced miner growled.

Billy Bray winced at the sudden pain and turned away, a look of inexpressible sadness on his face.

"You would roar, too," he answered. "Yes, you'd roar if you felt my load." Then, facing them, he cried fiercely, "And roar I will, until I get it off!"

The load was heavy. Strong drink binds almost unbreakable chains around a victim. The habits of years must be broken, but Billy Bray had help, and eagerly he took advantage of it.

Joey, of course, noted the difference in her husband. But she had been fooled too often to really hope for Billy's change to be permanent.

Payday came. Joey prepared supper as usual, never once dreaming that Billy would be home. He never was on payday. Always when he did arrive home, drunk and befuddled, he had little money left for her and the children.

To her joy and surprise, Billy opened the door and stepped in—sober. He may have stopped and bought the children some sweets, or purchased a piece of choice meat for the soup pot, but his money that day did not go into the alehouse till.

Joey ran to him. "O Billy!" she cried, hardly able to believe her eyesight. "Billy, how is it you're home so early tonight?"

Billy stood up straight. His mouth took on resolute lines; his eyes shone with determination. "You will never see me drunk again, Joey, by the help of the Lord. He can cure drunkards."

The house seemed suddenly different to Joey. She straightened the bare little room and put the children to bed.

Billy had gone upstairs. Kneeling by the bed, he prayed till Joey came upstairs. A change had begun in both of them. During those first few days he spent many hours with the Bible and the hymn-book, rejoicing at the promises in one and the assurance of the other. Charles Wesley's lovely poems were balm to his aching heart.

> "Depth of Mercy! can there be
> Mercy still reserved for me?
> Can my God His wrath forbear—
> Me, the chief of sinners, spare?
>
> . . . . .
>
> "There for me the Saviour stands,
> Shows His wounds and spreads His hands;
> God is love! I know, I feel;
> Jesus weeps and loves me still."

Billy Bray pleaded for mercy and forgiveness. He said, I was glad I had begun to seek the Lord, for it is said, 'Let the heart of them rejoice that seek the Lord.'

The first Sunday arrived. Full of happiness and hope, Billy and Joey set out for the chapel a mile from their house where the Bible Christians had class meeting. It was a miserable day, rainy and chilly, but they went just the same.

Satan was determined to discourage Billy if he could. That first day, when he had hoped for so much in fellowship, he received nothing. Not a soul came, much to Billy's disappointment. Plodding home, he tried to understand how people could stay away from an appointment with the Lord for such a trivial reason. "If a little rain will keep the people away from the house of God, I shall not join here," he decided. He changed his mind later when he realized that people's neglect must not exert too much influence. To God he reached out, not to men.

On Monday afternoon he returned to his regular work shift at the mine, still battling his load of sin, still not completely comprehending God's promises. The awful fear that he would not find mercy, that he had gone too far in the realm of evil to find peace, bore down upon him.

Joey tried to tempt him with food. Her pasties baked sizzling and brown in the brick oven, but Billy did not care to cat. The tea cakes and puddings, fashioned by her anxious, loving hands, remained untasted.

He came home from the mine at eleven that night, still sad, distraught, and in agony. He had begun to understand how frightful it is to be lost, but as yet the power, glory, and joy of salvation had not come into his realization.

Nearly that whole night he spent on his knees. He knew perfectly well what a wretched life he had led. It did not seem possible he could obtain mercy so easily. Satan saw what a formidable foe Billy Bray would be once he had completely accepted the gospel of Jesus Christ. He determined Billy should never have that experience.

Later when he talked about those hours loaded with agony and anxiety, Billy commented, I was glad that I had begun to seek the Lord, for I felt I would rather be crying for mercy than living in sin."

The next afternoon in the darkness of the mine, while he worked hard with his pick and shovel, it seemed that the devil himself stood beside him. "You'll never find mercy, Billy, never!" the voice hissed.

"Thou art a liar, Devil!" Billy shouted to the air in front of him.

Instantly the load lifted from his heart. He had unconsciously fulfilled one of the commands of God, "Resist the devil, and he will flee from you"—and the promise was fulfilled immediately. He praised God for his deliverance.

His companions ridiculed his habit of praising the Lord, begun in the darkness of the mine, but that did not stop him.

"I am not so happy as some, but sooner than I would go back to sin again, I would be put in that 'plat' [an open space near the shaft of a mine] there, and burned to death," he explained.

Again that night he walked past the table prepared with so much anxiety and thought by Joey. But a different look shone on Billy's face now. Before, his anguish of heart and spirit had been fearful. Tonight it seemed as if the door of heaven had been pushed open just a crack, and he had had a glimpse of the indescribable glory that could be his for the taking. What was supper, with heaven Just ahead? Billy hungered and thirsted after God's acceptance, His favor.

Joey was anxious, but with a different anxiety than before. She followed him to the stairs, but now she saw a man go upstairs seeking his God.

Upstairs, Billy, with the wonder of his afternoon victory still upon him, found himself more confident. Beautifully and touchingly, he described the scene:

"I said to the Lord, 'Thou hast said, "They that ask shall receive, they that seek shall find, and to them that knock the door shall be opened," and I have faith to believe it.'"

In that instant such happiness flooded his soul that he could never afterward express exactly how he felt.

CHAPTER FIVE

NOVEMBER in Cornwall is a cold, damp, dreary month. Thick fogs, chilling and penetrating, press down over streets, rolling and billowing over lanes, fields, and villages, sweeping in from the cold, lashing waters of the North Atlantic.

But Billy Bray always particularly remembered that bleak November in 1823. It spelled freedom and the first real happiness be had ever known. He was always amazed that others could not see the door to happiness he had found, so clear and plain it seemed to him.

To Billy's amazement his conversion changed everything for him. Even the trees looked more beautiful; the streets and the houses sparkled with life; his wife looked lovelier, too. He gazed in wonder at everything as if he had been transported into a new world and granted newer, better eyesight. Some said he was touched in the head. Billy asserted that he had been touched in the heart.

Later, Billy proudly told people, "They said I was a *mad*-man, but they meant I was a *glad*-man, and...have been glad ever since!"

Friends and neighbors tried to "bring Billy to his senses." Billy became increasingly amazed at their logic.

"Bringing me to my *senses*, indeed!" he thought angrily. "When I was in what they believed was 'my senses,' I wasted my wages in the wine shops, and allowed my wife and children to live in poverty. When I was 'in my senses,' I blasphemed, derided God, was gone from home most of the time, went on such drunken sprees that I had snakes in my boots. I stole, frittered money away on gambling, and spent my time with low companions. So *that* is what they are trying to return me to!" he exclaimed. Well, he had another idea.

All attempts to change Billy rolled off him like water. Determined that nothing could reason him out of his convictions or rob him of his peace and hope, he waged a fearful battle with his habits of cursing, lying, stealing, drinking, and neglect. But his reward grew increasingly sweeter. He knew more surely the might of salvation's gift, which faith in the Lord Jesus Christ had given him. It filled him with a peculiar rapture that would always be the lodestone of his quaintly trustful life.

CHAPTER SIX

JOEY WAS Billy's first convert. At Hicks Mill Chapel she regained her lost Christian experience.

The chapel, built first through the generosity of Thomas Tregaskis in 1821, became so popular that it soon outgrew its original dimensions and had to be enlarged. A great squarish building, it had no architectural beauty; yet during the years when the Bible Christians labored there, many precious souls gave their hearts to Jesus Christ. Joey was one of these.

Billy's influence soon spread down into the mine where he worked. Before, the men had relied on him to provide laughs with his vulgar jokes or ridiculous remarks. Now all was changed.

Billy knew that some of the miners who before had encouraged his jokes and laughed at them were professed Christians. Now he wondered why they had never taken the pleasure in praying that he had. Danger of cave-ins and gas explosions lurked in every mine. Many a man has gone beneath the earth in the morning never to return. Realizing their need of prayer, Billy braved their black looks and sneering remarks, and started the habit of praying with those who would, before they went down the dark, dank tunnels to their long day of back-breaking work. "Now, if you will hearken to me," Billy would say, "I will pray for you before we go to work, for if I did not pray with you, and any of us should be killed, I should think it was my fault."

"You pray, Billy, and we'll listen," one of the men ventured to reply.

Billy understood their feelings of reticence. He decided to pray in such simple language that even the dullest could see a clear way before him. He prayed, "Lord, if any of us must be killed, or die today, let it be *me*; let not one of these men die, for they are not happy; but I am, and if I die today, I shall go to heaven."

Whenever Billy arose from his knees, he noticed tears on the cheeks of the hardened miners. It was not long until Billy had them praying, too.

Billy, lighting his candle of faith, resolved that it would always radiate light to all in the house. His religion was not a safety lamp, saved until be should be going down into the dark valley, nor a chapel gaslight that burned only on Sundays and at evening services. Once lighted, his faith was perhaps put into a commonplace candlestick, but everyone around him could see by it. One thing about his lighted candle Billy never forgot—it burned none the less for every new candle lighted from it.

Down in the mine, William, an old unconverted man, worked near Billy. The man's son also worked there, and Billy had a great burden for their happiness and conversion—synonymous terms to the Cornish miner-preacher.

Billy kept at them all the time, telling them continually what the Lord wanted to do for them. Invariably he dropped to his knees and prayed for them whether they liked it or wanted the prayers.

He was gratified at times to see the old man's eyes fill with tears, but his hopes would be crushed before the day ended by bearing him swearing at his son. Billy was almost tempted at times to give up because the case seemed hopeless, but he didn't, so determined was he to outwit the devil.

Then the old man fell ill. Billy renewed his efforts to help him see Jesus in all His beauty, and his efforts were rewarded. The old lips, so used to cursing, now spoke praises and blessing. The man was changed completely and later died happy in Jesus. Billy had given him the "safety lamp" to light his stumbling feet through the shadowy valley.

CHAPTER SEVEN

AFTER his seven wicked years in Devonshire, when Billy had returned to Cornwall, he brought with him an old crony of drunkenness and devilment named Justin, After Billy's conversion, he began telling his comrades what danger they were in. They often called him a fool, playing mean tricks on him and persecuting him, trying to rouse in him the vile temper they well remembered.

When they did treat him unkindly, Justin, though still unconverted, flew fiercely to Billy's defense. Once be shouted, "You shall leave that man alone, and say nothing to him, for I knew him when he was a drunkard, and now he is a good man; I wish I was like him." Billy overheard this defense, and sorrow for his unsaved friend melted his heart.

Billy planted a garden near his home, which he tended outside of the hours he spent in the mine. His family lived better now. Out in the garden early in the morning, while dew still trembled on the cabbage leaves, he took his burdens to his Friend, the Lord Jesus Christ. Occasionally talking aloud, he pulled weeds, pulverized a clod or two, or perhaps picked marrows (a kind of squash) for Joey to cook.

One day he told the Lord about Justin and his longing to see his friend taste the spiritual sweetness be savored every day. Suddenly the Lord spoke into Billy's mind so convincingly that he shouted for joy. "I will save him soon," He had said.

A day or so later Billy saw his friend. "I have good news for you, J.T.," Billy told him joyfully.

"You have? What's that?" Justin inquired.

"The Lord told me you will be converted soon," Billy answered.

And soon Justin shared Billy's deep Christian happiness.

When God impressed Billy's heart to pray for someone in particular, he considered it a sure sign that the person would be converted.

Working in the mine with Billy was another man named William Bray. Perhaps a distant relative, the other Bray was also a very wicked man, plunged in every type of indulgence and evil. In November, 1823, the month of Billy's conversion, the second William Bray became captain of the copper mine. Billy, in his characteristic way, said, "Both of us were promoted at the same time,...[but] I was adopted into the royal family of heaven, and made a child of God." Billy knew that his promotion was the greater.

Perhaps hearing of William's promotion started Billy to pondering about him, but more than likely he had one of those divinely inspired impressions from the Lord.

"One Monday evening," recounted Billy, "it was impressed on my mind that if I went to see him, he would be saved."

Billy did not delay, but went without a doubt in his mind that all would be well. He told him in his own inimitable and forthright manner what he had been impressed to do. Praying with him, he spoke from his own experience of the rich benefits that would be his if he relinquished the evils of the world and became one in thought and action with the Lord. It was too much for William Bray. The glory that Billy portrayed so graphically made the world and its pleasures shrink alarmingly, and William Bray found Christ.

The man became dangerously ill shortly after that, and Billy, with his keen insight, perceived that it was William's last illness. Visiting him many times, he found him filled with joy in Christ Jesus.

Just before he passed away, he had someone go after Billy, saying he had a message for him. When Billy came into the room, William's face lighted up. "I wanted to tell you," he said, seizing Billy's hand, "that Christ is *mine*." Billy must have shouted with gladness, for it is said that the dying man did also, the thought of being one with Christ filling him with holy ecstasy.

The mines drew a family of Irish Catholics named Burns into Cornwall, and providentially into Twelveheads, a little too near to dynamic Billy Bray for comfort. To Mrs. Burns's fury, he would hop and skip right into her house, singing,

"Lord, save this dear little Irish woman." Mrs. Burns detested Billy Bray and dreaded to see him coming. He was so forthright and enthusiastic about Christ that one could not ignore him. She simply had to endure his vociferous comings and goings.

The hammering campaign eventually brought results. Mrs. Burns saw her neighbors changed because of the revival work fostered by Billy Bray and his friends. She would have had to be exceedingly stupid to ignore it. Quite suddenly she began to attend the meetings, and before long she became a devoted Bible Christian.

CHAPTER EIGHT

W. HASLAM, in Cornwall, was a proud and eminent clergyman. His church was well ordered and decorous, and he continually cherished a feeling of self-satisfaction about the dignity of his labors. He would have been horrified if someone had told him he was a lost man. But the Lord used one of his servants, a humble gardener, to show him he needed to be soundly converted himself before he could attempt to lead a spiritual flock to the Lord.

When his gardener fell critically ill with galloping consumption, it soon became plain that nothing could be done to save his life. When the servant faced the knowledge that be was soon to die, his heart almost failed him. Nothing in his religion seemed to comfort him in his dark hour. Nor could the minister bring peace to his soul, though he tried hard.

Friends had told him of the peace of the Bible Christians, against whom he had often heard Haslam preach. He had heard the details of their deep joy over sins forgiven.

The dying man shook his head sadly. The cultured and dignified religion he professed gave him no such assurance. In his agony he sent for one of the preachers of whom his master so highly disapproved.

Haslam tried to tell his servant that all was well, that be might be assured, with his good life and profession, of entrance into God's kingdom.

The Bible Christian preacher did just the opposite. Instead of comforting him, he assured the sick man he *was* indeed lost, pointing out that nothing he himself had done would save him. Christ alone can save. "Now, pray for yourself," he confidently told him.

When the dying gardener found peace in Jesus, his pastor, instead of rejoicing with him, was angered at the interference from men he haughtily considered his inferiors. Again and again the gardener sent for him, but in his hardness of heart he refused several urgent invitations.

When at last he did consent to go, he endeavored to make the man return to his former views; but polite acquiescence had no part in a life soon to be over. The sick gardener awaited eternity. He could not be shaken from his faith.

The gardener being so close to death, Haslam expected to find him in bed. But be found him walking about the room, praising God and fairly trembling with joy.

"Ah, John, you are excited!" exclaimed his pastor. "You have been taking wine!"

"No, master," John replied, "I have not touched a drop of it—no, dear no, that is not it, dear master. I know you love me and I love you—you don't know this joy and peace, I am sure you don't, or you would have told me of it. O master! pray the Lord to give it to you. I will never rest praying for you. Don't be angry with me. The Lord bless you and convert your soul!"

This was too much for the eminent clergyman, who had convinced himself suavely that he was perfectly all right. But the break had been made. In his distress he visited a brother clergyman, who told him bluntly that if he had been truly converted, he would not have been angered at John's conversion. Rather, he would have rejoiced when the man found peace and happiness in Christ.

Haslam immediately realized that to see souls converted in his parish, he must first know conversion himself. When the bell rang for the church service the following Sunday, he trembled at the thought of standing before the people, knowing his unreadiness to minister to them.

In the midst of his discourse on the words "What think ye of Christ?" he found conversion. Suddenly it came to his heart that the church with its form and ritual did not provide the answer. It was merely a means of leading souls to its head, Jesus, the Lamb of God.

So filled was he with spirit and joy that his fervor infected his entire congregation. Many members examined their lives during the meeting, and many found the relationship they needed to have with Christ.

Just as soon as Billy Bray heard of this heart-warming experience, he announced, "I'd like to see that man, to give my eyes a treat."

Expressing a mutual desire, the minister said, "I had often heard of Billy Bray at Baldhu, from his brother James, and wished very much to see him. One morning, three months after my conversion, I heard someone walking about in the hall of my house, praising the Lord."

A bit surprised, Haslam rose from the break-fast table to investigate who had entered his house so unceremoniously. He saw a small man with a radiant countenance.

"Who are you, sir?"

Billy's face shone with the glory of his belief. "I am Billy Bray—be ye the 'passon'?"

"Yes," Haslam told him.

"Converted, be ye?"

"Yes, thank God."

"Be the missus converted?"

"Yes."

"Thank the dear Lord," he said fervently, his face beaming with smiles. He bowed to the minister's wife.

"Be there any maids in this house?"

"Yes, there are three," answered Mrs. Haslam.

"Are they converted?"

"Yes."

"Where be they?"

When she told him they were in the kitchen, he had to go there immediately. It was as if he could not miss a chance to greet every relative he had in the family of God. It wasn't long till shouts of praise to God penetrated to the dining room, where the family still sat at breakfast.

When Billy returned to the dining room, they invited him to eat breakfast with them. But the unpredictable Billy suddenly approached the minister, and though he was a fairly big man, Billy picked him up and trotted around the table with him in his arms, so happy was he. After he set the gentleman on his chair, he rolled on the floor for pure joy.

Finally Haslam persuaded his excited guest to eat breakfast, for Billy had been riding in a slow-moving donkey cart since midnight to get there, and as it was January, it was cold in Cornwall.

Billy had a special reason for being eager to see the Haslams. He told them the story of a prayer now being answered through their conversion.

Several years before, Billy had been near Haslam's parish, before the house where the parson now lived had even been erected. When he passed over the spot where the house now stood, he was, as usual, communing with the Lord. "I will give thee all that dwell on this mountain," spoke the gentle Voice in Billy's ear.

Instantly the little Cornish preacher knelt down and prayed for those who lived there.

Billy wasn't one to sit back and wait for God to answer his prayers. He set out to visit those in every house again and again persistently, until he brought every one to Christ.

Like Alexander the Great, who wept after be had conquered the world and had nothing left to conquer, after Billy had conquered the enemy, he lamented the fact that there were only three houses on that hill. Billy listened intently for the answers to his prayers. He was told that there would be more converts. He never forgot the hill, for he considered it a heritage from the Lord. He waited patiently for news of more converts as the Lord had promised.

Then one day he heard from his brother James that a church, a parsonage, and a school were being built on the place that the Lord had plainly promised to him. Always delighted with the wonderful ways the Lord has of bringing His promises to pass, Billy leaped joyfully at the news. He must have toted half the town of Twelveheads around in his arms in his glee. Every day he waited eagerly for more news.

Then James wrote back discouraging news: a "Pusey" had been appointed to preach in that beloved place.

Billy instantly recognized the significance of the term "Pusey," and his buoyant spirits sank to zero and congealed.

At this time a religious faction was making an effort to edge the Anglican Church closer to the Catholic concept of what the church should be. In

1833 an English clergyman, E. B. Pusey, sought to strengthen the position of the Anglican Church by returning to the doctrine and ritual of the seventeenth century when it had seemed to make a greater impact on the minds of the people. Pusey was a member of the Oxford Movement, a group that formed because of a fear that many people would join the Catholic Church as a reaction against the liberalization of the Church of England. Some of Pusey's followers opposed evangelical Protestantism.

Thus when Billy learned that a follower of Pusey—with his emphasis on ritual and the importance of the institutional church above that of its members—had come to pastor the church on the hill which meant so much to Billy, he felt bitterness in his heart.

Then when Billy received the news of the "Pusey's" change of heart and life, he wanted to go immediately and see that "passon and his missus," as he called them in his dialect, to rejoice with them over the change in their lives.

CHAPTER NINE

BILLY DID NOT follow any set pattern in his preaching. He did what he felt was the best for the given occasion. Often it meant reciting a stanza from a hymn, telling a story, or recounting a personal experience.

He pleased the people; and wherever he preached, rich and poor, small and great, crowded in to hear the Cornish miner with the vibrant personality. His popularity was such that his name became a household word throughout Cornwall.

A little wizened wiry man, Billy Bray had burning, darting eyes under determined brows, eyes that would have been almost fierce and frightening if they had not been set in the midst of smile —crinkles. The firm mouth that never once gave a hint of vacillation or weakness perpetually smiled. There was a beauty about his countenance hard to describe.

He always wore a black suit with a white tie, the accepted mode of dress for the minister, and Billy looked the part. Yet a difference made one look again. If he talked to you a moment, you could be sure he would begin to inquire about your soul. If the reply was affirmative and assured, Billy was not ashamed of shouting for joy in a busy street or a country lane. This habit became accepted after he made his reputation. Cornwall and Devonshire knew Billy Bray.

Billy's illustrations were most convincing. At one time he preached to a large congregation, mostly miners. Billy knew mining, and he knew they did. He was one of them, and they loved him.

In the neighborhood were located two mines. The miners received excellent pay at the prosperous one. The other had poor working conditions and poor pay.

By way of illustration, Billy represented himself to be an employee of the poor mine. When payday came, he pretended, he decided to go to the good mine to collect his wages. The incongruity of the situation amused the miners. He carried on the imaginary conversation he would have with the puzzled paymaster, who did not recognize him. Of course, he would be asked if he had not been working over at the other mine—the shabby, decrepit mine that paid such low wages. "Yes," answered Billy, frankly, naively, but I like the wages over here far better, so I've decided to draw my wages here."

In vain he pleaded and argued with, and cajoled, the paymaster. But it did no good. He was told to get out, and informed that if he ever expected any pay from that mine, he must come and work there.

Billy turned to the intent congregation, who drank in his easily understood illustrations, and brought out his point so adroitly that the smallest child could understand. He told of the Saviour who offers glories, victories, and joy, endless and eternal, if we but work for Him. His rewards to those serving Him are infinitely better than the wages from a fine and prosperous mine.

The devil pays wages too, Billy pointed out—frightful, horrible wages—and to him they must resort for their pay if they give their lives to his service. A servant of the devil can never apply for the rewards of the faithful.

Billy had delightful ways of making texts live. He seemed to have an insight into the most graphic and expressive way of speaking. " 'I am the bread of life,' " he would read. Then looking up with shining eyes, he would exclaim, "Precious loaf, this! The patriarchs and prophets ate of this loaf, and never found a bit of crust about it. The apostles and martyrs ate of this loaf, too, for many long years, and never found a bit of 'vinny' [mold] in it. And, bless the Lord! poor old Billy Bray can eat it without teeth, and get fat on it!"

Billy Bray's fame as a speaker spread far. At the opening of Trecrogo Chapel in the Launceston circuit, the people came in such droves that the new chapel simply would not hold them. Obliged to move out into the open fields, people sat on their coats and shawls on the ground.

Billy always had to take a slash at drunkenness in nearly every discourse. Since his subject at the Trecrogo Chapel that day had been announced to be "Happiness," he struck out at what had caused a great deal of sorrow and unhappiness in his own life. He always flew to the defense of the Christian life, as if someone might question whether or not a Christian had anything to be happy about. Billy's face belied that. He beamed when he exclaimed, "You may think we have nothing to drink, but we have." And to prove it he would quote Isaiah 25:6: "In this mountain shall the Lord of hosts make unto all people a feast of fat things, a feast of wines on the lees." "My Father keeps a wine shop," he would triumph.

His humble illustrations did not sound crude, nor were they calculated to get a laugh out of his listeners. Billy's love for all things holy seemed to glorify his use of humble things.

CHAPTER TEN

BILLY BRAY was a contemporary of Sir Humphry Davy, whose experiments with explosive gases in mines led to his invention of the safety lamp. After that, miners had no fear of the accidents resulting from firedamp in mines. As fine as the miner's cap was regarded then, Billy often told the men, "It will be a good thing to change a miner's hat for a crown."

"Oh, you western men!" he would cry, for he knew them like the back of his own hand. "I am an old miner. Come to heaven! If there is one crown short, I will willingly go without one!"

For Billy Bray to say that meant a great depth of love, for he longed with all his impetuous, eager spirit to see, live, and reign with the Lord, and to experience the glories he had so often dreamed about. He continually told his hearers with great confidence, "There is no want there." Billy had known want, hunger, cold, and nakedness, and his hands showed the hard calluses of grueling toil. He knew how to reach the common people, because he was one of them.

Preaching once at a town called Devonport, he said in his droll manner, "We hear a good deal nowadays about what is called 'Baptismal Regeneration'; I don't know what it is, but I tell 'ee, friends, if it'u'd make me happier, I'd go into it like a duck-head, wings, feathers, and all."

Billy had little patience with critical Christians, with those not willing to do anything themselves nor to allow others any freedom. His sarcasm for such people found expression in apt, yet homely, illustrations.

"You people here ha'n't got half so much sense as the ducks home wi' we," he said. "If we throw down a handful of corn, and there should be a little chaff among it, our ducks do eat up all the corn and leave all the chaff; but when you get your corn, you pick up all the chaff, and leave all the corn."

Leaving a home for a preaching appointment once, he said to his hostess, "Mary, shall us pray a bit?" Without waiting for her refusal or consent, Billy dropped down to his knees as if it were no more of a ceremony to wonder at than tying his shoe.

"We've nothing particular to ask Thee for, Lord, but go with Thy servant to K., and stay with these dear women, and bless them, Lord, and keep them right," he prayed.

He believed in praising the Lord constantly, doing so with great sincerity. He continually recounted to all who would listen God's wonderful works in his life, confident that it took these continual testimonials to drive back and limit the power of Satan and keep him under restraint. To one of his friends, Mr. Maynard, he often said as they left the house, "Now, friend Maynard, let us pray a minute before we go, or else the devil will be scratching me on the way. If I leave without praying, this is the way he serves me; but when I get on my knees a minute or two before leaving, I cut his old claws, and then he can't harm me; so I always like to cut his claws before I go."

Billy Bray was so original and naive in his worship and praise that even conservative people allowed Billy to get by with things of which they did not wholly approve.

An active Christian, he defined "deadness" as Christlessness. To the childlike heart of the humble miner, the joy of being one with Christ was so effervescent that he continually sang and shouted with happiness.

Billy had a friend, John, from Devonshire, who delighted in hearing him preach. But when the meeting turned into a typical Billy Bray praise service, accompanied with singing, shouting, and praying, then John would quietly retire and go home.

But one night a dream convinced John of Billy's deep sincerity, removing his prejudices. Thereafter he stayed at Billy's praise meetings. Indeed, he joined in gladly, his wholeheartedness moving even Billy.

When John died, someone heard Billy quaintly remark, "So he has done with the *doubters*, and is got up with the *shouters*."

To Billy Bray, religion had no sad side. He could never understand folk who went around with faces long enough to eat oats out of a chum. The only dark thing in his life was the sin he remembered doing before his conversion.

Even down in the inky blackness of the mine, when the idea of his oneness with Christ surged through him, his emotions welled over until he would leap and dance under the ground as well as on the surface.

"All that dancing and prancing and shouting is not religion," his former friends scoffed, trying to throw a wet blanket on his exuberance. "You don't have to make such a big fuss to show folks you've got religion."

But Billy was not shaken. Even though people told him there was no need of all that noise, since surely God was not hard of hearing, Billy had his answer ready. "I was born in the *fire*," he declared, "and could not live in the smoke." He told them that the devil had good ears too, but *his* servants certainly made a big racket, and made it plenty. He "would rather see us doubting than hear us shouting," he concluded in the droll way which usually silenced his critics.

Many places today would disapprove of Billy and frown upon him, even as long ago the more conservative folk did. Some people hurt his feelings, no doubt, for Billy was human and tenderhearted. He did not like sarcasm or carping criticism any better than we do today. When told that the scriptures he referred to were figurative, not literal, Billy protested loudly. The Bible was real, vivid, graphic. If David danced before the Lord with all his might, why couldn't Billy Bray?

Some people thought his meetings lacked dignity and reverence, but Billy would point out that the people of Israel "shouted with a great shout" at the laying of the foundation for the second temple.

One day Billy heard that his minister friend S. W. Christophers was sick. His friends and family thought he would not live. People tiptoed about the minister's house, and silence gripped the sufferer's bedroom.

Into this sad, uneasy atmosphere Billy bounced, full of the jubilant joy of being one with Christ and in tune with His will. His well-known "Hallelujah!" broke into the stillness. Even the sick man in the upstairs bedroom heard the triumphant cry. Then Billy dashed up the stairs, singing with all his humble heart.

Undoubtedly Billy's buoyant faith and fervent prayers contributed to his friend's recovery. Weeks later the man declared, "I was raised up to see and hear Billy again, many, many times."

CHAPTER ELEVEN

THE COUNTY of Cornwall has many churches, and it has been said that Methodism is the mother church of this sea-surrounded shire. The amazing thing is that a substantial number of them were built by the sacrificing efforts of the poor rather than by the rich. Such a condition came about through the efforts of John Wesley and many other humble, dedicated men similar to Billy Bray.

The county had not always been distinguished by people so enthusiastic for the work of God. Billy Bray delighted in recounting conditions as he saw them.

"In the neighborhood where I lived there were a great many dark-minded, wicked people, and chapels were few. The Lord put it into my mind to build a chapel. My mother had a small place; and by one of her little fields there was a small piece of common. The Lord opened my mother's heart to give a spot on that piece of common to build on. When my mother gave me the ground, I began to work as the dear Lord told me, and to take away the hedge of my mother's field, and to dig out the foundation for a chapel, or a house to worship God in, which was to be called *Bethel*....In that day there was but one little chapel in our neighborhood, at a place called Twelveheads, which belonged to the Wesleyans. Our people had a little old house to preach in, which would hold only twenty or thirty persons. So we wanted a place to preach in, and the people a place to hear in. Paul had a thorn in the flesh, and so had I. For I had not only the wicked against me, but a little class which was held in the house where we preached; most of them turned against me, and tried to set the preachers against me. But with all they could do, they could not hurt me, though they made me uneasy at times. When I had got out the foundation of the Lord's house, we had preaching on the foundation stone."

An observer told of the occasion, for Billy made the most of it. His enthusiasm at its height, he stood there with the people flocked about him, listening and watching.

"If this new chapel," he cried with a resonant ring in his voice, "which they say is to be called Bethel, stands one hundred years, and one soul be converted in it every year, there will be one hundred souls, and one soul is worth more than all Cornwall!"

Most of the people in the area sympathized with Billy's scheme to build a chapel, but one man who owned two horses gave Billy plenty of trouble. He said he would not give even a halfpenny toward the chapel that Billy was wasting so much effort in putting up. Of course, people eyed him, for he was only one against many who seconded Billy in his unselfish labors for the good of his neighborhood.

The man used his horses to drive the "whim" (hoist) at the mine. Shortly after that one of his horses became so lame in the field that his owner lost many days of work.

"Oh, that is because he would not give anything to Billy Bray's chapel." The simple people nodded at each other knowingly.

A small thing like that did not perturb Billy, nor was he superstitious. He passed the circumstance off by saying cryptically, "The people said that the horse was taken lame because the owner would not give anything to Billy Bray's chapel. But the people must know that it was not mine, but the dear Lord's chapel. And it may be the Lord punished him for not giving anything to *His* chapel."

Billy later sadly remarked concerning this matter: "The chapel was never much good to that man, for he died soon after; and the Lord enabled me to build the chapel without his help.... When I had taken down the field hedge, cleared out the foundation, had got some stone home to the place where the chapel was to be built, when the masons had put up some of the walls, and I had one pound fifteen shillings given me by friends, the devil entered into some of my classmates, who said that the chapel ought not to be built there."

How hard this must have been to a man living by faith. Every small advantage gained was, to Billy's trusting eyes, a definite providence of the Lord. Men who tried to stop his good work he viewed with the impatience and courage of a Nehemiah on the walls of Jerusalem. He said, "When my classmates saw that they could not stop me, they went to the superintendent of the circuit and told him that he ought to stop me from building the chapel there, for that was not the place; it ought to be built at Twelveheads or at Tippett's Stamps."

It seemed strange to the little preacher that those who had done little or nothing should try to hinder the work which he thought approved by the Lord. The work was hard and taxing enough without battling against unnecessary hindrances. But by this time Billy was used to the many and varied plans the devil uses to divert people from God's work.

The circuit preacher came solemnly to Billy and told him that the members had asked him to stop Billy from building the chapel.

"The Lord put it into my mind to build this chapel here," Billy replied simply. Then he led the circuit preacher around and showed him how high the walls were, and how sturdy the foundation. Since a great deal had been done, representing much hard work, planning, and praying, Billy's heart was thoroughly upset at the thought of stopping.

Since preaching was scheduled that night, the circuit leader diplomatically asked Billy if he would be willing to cast lots on the question. Surely he would like to inquire of the Lord whether or not to build the chapel there.

"Yes," answered Billy readily, I am willing to do that. I do not want to build the chapel here unless it is the Lord's will."

They wrote three names on slips of paper and put them into a container to be drawn: Twelveheads, Tippett's Stamps, and Cross Lanes, the latter being the place Billy had chosen.

His enemies were jubilant, confident of success, for they had two chances to Billy's one. Before the drawing they condescendingly assured him of their cooperation and help, not only in gathering stone, but in building the chapel as well.

The Lord did not forsake the mighty little man of faith. When they drew the lot, to his enemies' chagrin, it came out Cross Lanes, where Billy's chapel stood, already half built.

Those who had lavishly promised to help when they thought they might have their way, went back on their word, saying, "We shall not help you, for Cross Lanes is not the proper place."

Neither hurt, dismayed, nor discouraged, Billy just kept on with his work. He raised the stone, scouted around for enough mortar, and saw that the walls went steadily upward.

"The dear Lord helped me," Billy declared, "for I was very poor, and had no money of my own."

Miracles built the chapel. Billy expected this, knowing and trusting the Lord as he did. Enough money came in on time to pay the masons. When

Billy needed timber for the rafters, he left the problem with his heavenly Father. Billy simply asked for either the "principals" (roof trusses) or money enough to buy them.

He learned later that the same morning he prayed, the Lord set about to answer his prayer.

A local Wesleyan preacher was praying in his home. While he was on his knees, the Lord told him to go and give Billy Bray a pound note.

After he had eaten breakfast, he hurried down to Cross Lanes and found Billy already bard at work, getting ready for the timbers he knew would come.

Coming around to where Billy was working, he asked without preamble, "What do you want a pound note for?" Immediately Billy informed him of his need, Mating how he had told the Father about it. The minister shook his head in wonder. It was one thing to *read* of miracles, of instantaneous answers to prayer, and another to be directly involved in one of them.

"I never felt such a thing in my life," he declared, his voice filled with amazement. "While I was home praying this morning, it was always coming into my mind to go down and give you a pound note, and here it is."

Billy's soul thrilled at the graciousness of God in quickly answering his prayer. Off he went without a doubt, dancing and praising God, and bought the timber for the building.

As if he did not have enough trouble, sorrow and anxiety came into his own humble home at the same time. His wife agonized over their little girl's terrible illness. They spent day and night up with her. None of their simple home remedies seemed to help.

Satan began to work on Billy in these terrible hours of anxiety and tension. "It will take you seven pounds to finish that chapel, Billy, and you have only two," the devil reminded him. Billy had to agree with these hard facts. He knew the devil often prefaced some of his greatest lies with truth, to throw people off guard.

"Now, Billy, your little girl is going to die, and it's going to take a whole pound to bury her. That will take one of those pounds in your pocket, and you'll have only one left."

Billy sweat with agony. He knew he could use the pound in good conscience, for he and the Lord kept one purse. He had contributed more than two pounds from his work in the mine, stinting himself again and again, though he never touched money given him specifically for the building. That he considered holy.

The evil whispering depressed him with a grief and despair he seldom yielded to, until his buoyant faith, ever predominant, took over the reins of his thoughts.

"Why," he told himself wonderingly, "I'm building this chapel for the Lord, and I should be paid for it! All these promises apply to me." His faith bounced back.

"Because thou hast built this chapel, I will save thy child's life," came the answer as plain as an audible voice. Comforted, sure the Lord had spoken, Billy asked immediately, "Where is this coming from?"

"I am the God of Abraham, Isaac, and Jacob. Be nothing doubting; it is I, saith the Lord."

Billy's childlike faith could believe such assurances as this, even though every indication pointed unmistakably to the fact that the child would die.

He went straight home where Joey was working, red-eyed and sad. His countenance was so cheerful that his wife looked at him in silent amazement. Confidently he told her to cheer up.

"Our little girl will not die, Joey," he said gently. "The Lord has told me so."

But she shook her head. Sleepless nights and worry had turned her heart to water. "Don't say so!" she cried, with a burst of grief. "All the neighbors say she will die; she is so very ill."

Even though things looked dark and hopeless and it seemed as if the Lord had turned His face away, Billy still believed firmly. Even though death seemed near, he collected his miner's tools and cap and went to work. Still Billy prayed, though the devil worked hard trying his faith. When he came home, hopefully, the child was no better. She had not eaten a bite, and all that night she continued to be critically ill. Billy went to work again the next day, never wavering in his faith. That noon, when he came home, the dinner table had been set, and they had made the little girl a bed on the window seat. She seemed not one bit better.

Billy and his wife and children knelt in their humble little kitchen to pray. "Dear Lord," Billy began, "Thou hast said that my child shall live, but she has not eaten any meat yet."

Imagine their joy, when they arose from their knees, to see the little girl sitting up. The window seat was close to the table. The little hands had the plate full, and she was spooning up food.

Billy must have attracted a lot of attention dancing and praising God all the way to the mines that afternoon.

Nothing delighted him so much as marked evidence of God's intervention.

"She is living now," Billy testified gleefully long afterward, "and is the mother of ten children; so the Lord made the devil a liar once more. The devil did not do me any hurt; he only made me bolder."

The problem of the seven pounds needed to fix the church still troubled him. The common purse of Billy and the Lord contained only two. He needed reeds to thatch the roof, but he was never a sluggard to ask the Lord for a thing, then sit down and wait for it to come.

Billy borrowed a horse and rode up among the farms where thatching reeds grew. Inquiring about their price, he learned reeds sold at two pounds for a hundred sheaves. He needed three hundred, requiring four pounds more, but he could laugh at that small difficulty in the face of what the Lord had just done for him.

When the farmer delivered the first hundred, Billy paid on the spot and asked for the other two hundred to be delivered just as soon as possible. That took faith, for only a few coins remained. But Billy trusted, and as always, God rewarded his faith. The money was there to pay when the rest were delivered.

The thatcher agreed to do the work of covering the church for one pound ten shillings. Billy looked into the purse, finding only one pound. He lacked ten shillings.

He stood there, pondering, watching the man high up on the gabled roof doing the intricate work of Dutch thatching.

Suddenly the overwhelming impression came over him to go to the highroad crowded with many people going and coming. He did not hesitate. Away he went, confident that it was the Lord's doing.

The first person he met was an acquaintance. "P.B.," he said, "you have not given me anything yet toward my Father's house."

The man stopped and frowned at the little preacher.

"No; nor do I intend to," he snapped. Billy looked steadfastly into the stubborn face. His look of confidence and faith remained.

"What are you 'amind' for the Lord to say to you in that day?" he inquired. "Do you want Him to say, 'You saw Me hungered, and you gave Me no meat: thirsty, and you gave Me no drink: a stranger, and you took Me not in: naked, and you clothed Me not'?"

This was too much for P.B. His face softened. You could not long be hard with Billy Bray. "Well," he hesitated, I don't mind if I do give you ten shillings."

Billy's face shone. "That is just the money I want!" he declared. Faith triumphant again, Billy hurried home, praising God.

After the provision of the principals and thatch, Billy became concerned with the finishing of the chapel. He needed wood for the door, the windows, and the seats inside.

A mine nearby had lately closed, and the owners were selling off the timber from the place. Billy checked at the mine and found just what he needed for a pound and six shillings, a large sum in those days. Billy's well-known faith inspired others to be on the lookout for bargains for his project, too.

"Billy, have you gone over to the mine to see what they have in the way of timber?" a friend inquired.

"Aye, and I have," he answered simply. "But I cannot buy yet. I have not the money."

The friend gave him a pound, and others added to it until he was able to buy the lumber. No sooner had he made the purchase than another difficulty became apparent. How would he get the lumber to Cross Lanes? Certainly he could not carry it on his back. He needed a horse and wagon for this.

"I've got a horse, but she's no good," a neighbor said, doubtfully. "She won't draw anything."

"Lend her to me," Billy replied. "I'll see if she'll do a bit of work for the Lord."

Away Billy went, leading the supposedly worthless horse. He hitched her to a cart and hauled all of the timber he had bought at the mine.

He could hardly make the neighbor believe that the horse had worked for him and had drawn the cart loaded heavy with timber from the mine to Cross Lanes. "I never saw a better horse in my life," he declared. "I did not touch her with whip or stick, though we had steep hills to come up over.

Billy had an apt explanation of the phenomenon. "That mare was working that day for a very strong company, Father, Son, and Holy Ghost, whom horses, angels, men, and devils must obey. If there had been no one there more powerful than Billy Bray, she would have been as bad with him as with anybody else."

Bethel became a success from the beginning. People thronged to it, until soon it was far too small to accommodate those who came seeking help. The congregation erected a larger Bethel next to the older one so bitterly contested by those who cast stumbling blocks in Billy's way. But his faith had made them into stepping-stones.

I have made you instrumental in building Bethel Chapel," God told him, "and I will make you the instrument in building one at Kerley Downs."

The honor placed upon him by the Lord of heaven and earth overjoyed Billy.

The believers there had gathered money for the chapel, but someone else bought the site they chose at a higher price. Discouraged, they continued meeting in someone's home.

It took Billy to find a spot for the chapel, to dig in with all the energy he had and get it built. Few people helped him, He had to labor daily in the mines in order to support his wife and five small children. Yet every moment he could spare, he went about his Master's business.

Many speaking appointments at widely separated places filled his Sundays. Frequently Billy would walk as much as twenty miles a day, besides preaching.

Then there was his garden; with the mine, the chapel, and his home responsibilities, Billy never had a leisure moment. Yet the Lord blessed him with abundant health, even when he often labored twenty out of the twenty-four hours.

"Had not the Lord helped me, I could not have done it," he explained. "Bless and praise His holy name."

CHAPTER TWELVE

BILLY BRAY took great pleasure in every Bible account of the life of our Lord, especially the happy parts. They rang an answering note in his vibrant personality. When he read the different passages describing Christ's triumphal entry into Jerusalem, he could hardly contain his enthusiasm.

He would read, "And a very great multitude spread their garments in the way; others cut down branches from the trees, and strawed them in the way. And the multitudes that went before, and that followed, cried, saying, Hosanna to the son of David: Blessed is he that cometh in the name of the Lord; Hosanna in the highest."

Billy would wonder indignantly, since people would shout for kings, or even ministers and governors in times of election, why couldn't *he* shout about Jesus? He was always aware of an undercurrent of scorn and criticism. It must have hurt his gentle heart, for he loudly and firmly justified the outbursts of praise, which he could not help.

He would scorn the mad excitement and fevered shouts at election time, declaring, "if this is worth shouting for, our election is worth far more, for those who get elected and sent up to the

House of Commons may soon die, or lose their seat at the next election;...but, if we get elected into...the Parliament House of Heaven, we shall never die, never get turned out; hence we have more reason to shout than they."

The Holy Bible was so real, such a treasure, that Billy relived every narrative. His humble, darting blue eyes never saw the world beyond the rough mine dumps and the fields of Devonshire and Cornwall, yet with deep spiritual insight he walked each day with Jesus as he pored over Holy Scripture.

He loved the account of Jesus healing the lame man lying at the Gate Beautiful. Some of his friends believed that this was the most beloved of all the Bible stories to the heart of the little Cornish preacher. Perhaps he felt such a kinship with anyone so happy that he jumped and ran as did that man who had always been a cripple.

Always alert, he saw the mercies of God everywhere. One of the sweetest traits of Billy's character was his precious tendency to be continually counting his blessings.

He ran joyfully into a friend's house in the city of Devonport one time. No one was too surprised since this was his normal way. He fairly shouted his praises to the Lord. "I have just seen a poor man down here with crutches and useless legs, and I haven't been able to help praising the Lord ever since for my sound ones," he explained.

A friend walked with him once when Billy was quite an old man. As usual, the conversation centered on heaven and the saints' reward. Billy stopped suddenly, as if overcome by the enormity and blessedness of his thoughts. His face filled with joy, and his old blue eyes brimmed with tears. "Praise the Lord!" he cried. Then suddenly he started to run, as lightly as a bushbuck or a deer. When his friend finally caught up with him, he was still thanking the Lord aloud. Turning his eyes on his friend, he said, "My dear brother, if I truly lived up to my privilege, I should not feel the ground over which I walk!" Billy could hardly bear to be earthbound. He strained violently at the leashes of mortality every day, longing intensely for heaven and Jesus.

When seventy years old, he attended a district meeting at a place called Hicks Mill. The speaker told about a good woman who had recently died, triumphant in her faith in Christ Jesus, her last word the exultant cry, "Victory!"

Billy listened carefully, the incident so touching his heart that he shouted, "Glory! If a *dying* woman praised the Lord, I should think a *living* man might."

The story is told that one day a host invited Billy to sit down and rest in the parlor until dinner was ready. As he led Billy to a chair in the quiet room, he remarked somewhat laughingly, "You won't find anything in this room to praise the Lord about. It's very plain and commonplace."

Billy looked around curiously. His host had left him alone in the room. Suddenly the family heard the little minister praising the Lord loudly. Puzzled, they hurried into the room. Billy had found an old geography book and had been reading. "It says here, he told them, "that the ocean is many miles deep in some places. And I know well if the Lord buried my sins in the depths of the sea, I'll not be bothered with them anymore."

CHAPTER THIRTEEN

CERTAINLY Billy had his trials, for he had to contend with deep poverty. We know very little about this, for his faith in his Father assured his simple soul that his needs would all be taken care of, and he did not consider his trials worth mentioning.

His temptations were great, and at times of stress Billy would in his exasperation rail out against the devil himself. "What an old fool thee art now; I have been battling with thee for twenty-eight years, and I have always beat thee, and I always shall."

Billy had to plant and plow and labor hard to sustain his family. Even so, he considered the Lord's work the supreme object of his whole life.

At one time, after he had toiled hard in his small plot, his potato crop suffered a blight and was a total failure. His whole crop was nothing but a small heap of scabby potatoes. Billy, humanly enough, had a brief moment of discouragement, wondering if the Lord did indeed love him. Satan pointed out that if the Lord loved him as much as he thought, he'd have had a bumper crop.

Billy told of the experience in these inimitable words: "Friends, last week I was a-diggin' up my 'taturs. It was a wisht poor yield, sure 'nough; there was hardly a sound one in the whole lot. An' while I was a-diggin', the devil come to me, and he says, 'Billy, do you think your Father do love you?'

"'I should reckon He do,' I says.

"'Well, I don't,' says the ould tempter in a minute. If I'd thought about it, I shouldn't ha' listened to 'en, for his 'pinions heen't worth the leastest bit o' notice. 'I don't,' says he, 'and I tell 'ee what for: if your Father loved you, Billy Bray, He'd give you a pretty yield o' 'taturs; so much as ever you do want, and ever so many of 'em, and every one of 'em as big as your fist. For it heen't no trouble to your Father to do anything; and He could just as easy give you plenty as not, an' if He loved you, He would, too.'

"Of course I wasn't goin' to let he talk o' my Father like that, so I turned round 'pon 'en.

"'Pray, sir,' says I, 'who may you happen to be, comin' to me a-talkin' like this here? If I heen't mistaken, I know you, sir, and my Father, too. And to think o' you comin ' a-sayin' He don't love me! Why, I've got your written character home to my house; and it do say, sir, that you be a liar from the beginnin'! An' I'm sorry to add, that I used to have a personal acquaintance with you, some years since, and I served you faithful as any poor wretch could; and all you gave me was nothing but rags to my back, and a wretched home, and an achin' head, an' no 'taturs, and the fear o' hellfire to finish up with. And here's my dear Father in heaven. I have been a poor servant of His, off and on, for thirty years. An' He's given me a clean heart, an' a soul full o' joy, an' a lovely suit o' white as'll never wear out; and He says that He'll make a king o' me before He've done, and that He'll take me home to His palace to reign with Him for ever and ever. An' now you come up here a-talkin' like that.'

"Bless 'ee, my dear friends, he went off in a minute, like as if he'd been shot—*I do wish he had—and he never had the manners to say 'good mornin'.'*"

When Billy prayed for the sick or ministered to the dying, he would always tell them he hoped to see them in heaven. Then he would add happily to those around the bedside that he had a personal reason in wishing to see them there. "If I saw them there, I must be there myself too." Then as if to excuse himself, he would add, "They say that every man has got a little self-thought, and so have I, too, for—

> "'I long to be there, His glory to share,
>   And to lean on Jesus' breast.'"

Heaven to Billy was nothing vague, shadowy, or ethereal. He visualized it and talked as casually of it as he would of Tavistock, Truro, or Twelveheads.

Once when they knelt to pray, Billy, to whom Jesus was so precious, cried with great feeling, "The blood! the blood!! the precious blood!!! the precious, precious blood!!!!" The effect on the whole company was instantaneous. Christ and His sacrifice meant more to the little Cornish preacher than life itself.

He always urged people to loosen the binding chains of pride and fear, and praise the Lord. It was an antidote to all evil for Billy Bray. He thought that complimenting the Lord had its mighty values. "I can't help praising the Lord. As I go along the meet, I lift up one foot, and it seems to say 'Glory!' and I lift up the other, and it seems to say 'Amen'; and so they keep on like that all the time I'm walking."

CHAPTER FOURTEEN

BILLY and a man called T. A. once were doing some special work in the Penzance circuit. The family with whom they stayed gave him and the very conservative T. A. a room and a bed together. Anyone who ever entertained Billy Bray had learned to expect almost anything from the enthusiastic little man.

Very early the next morning, wiry Billy leaped out of bed and began jumping, dancing, singing, and praising his God as usual, displeasing the man in the bed. To him, it was a breach of good behavior to sing and shout so loud in a quiet, sleeping household. But his protests had no effect at all.

"Oh, they can lie and sleep, and let their wheels get rusty if they want to," Billy retorted, shouting louder than before. "But I'm going to see to it that my wheels are kept nicely oiled and ready for work!"

With that, Billy got down on his knees and with all the fervor he could muster, prayed for the whole household. It is certain no one remained asleep by that time. He finished with a special exhortation and supplication for T. A., his disapproving bedfellow. "Lord, have mercy on T. A.," he prayed, loud enough to be heard all over the house, to the man's discomfiture. "Make him a better man than he appears to be," he requested of the Lord.

Billy always tried to attend any important church gatherings. One day a big anniversary rally met at Tywardreath Highway Chapel. People packing the place jammed it so that even little Billy Bray had to wedge and squeeze to get himself in.

An instance such as this delighted the heart of the preacher. He loved every evidence of loyalty to God. "Bless the Lord!" he sang out in his familiar high-pitched voice, "little Billy Bray is come once more to Highway."

"Billy Bray is here!" The message went through the crowd like an electric current. A path immediately cleared for him up to the pulpit, and he fairly leaped and danced his way there, singing his little doggerel.

When he announced the hymn, he read the first line of it. As there were few books in those days, sometimes ministers and elders had to line it out for the congregation to sing.

"'Oh, for a thousand tongues to sing,'" he read. Looking over the audience, he smiled. "Just think!" he said; "that's nine hundred and ninety-nine more than I've got!"

That day when Billy started for home, he had as a companion a young boy named Johnny. Billy patted the boy on the shoulder and looked back at the crowd as they walked away. "Johnny and I, we'll make the valleys ring with our singing and praising as we go home!"

Someone inquired, "Then you are a singer, Billy?"

"Oh, yes," cried the little preacher. "Bless the Lord! I can sing. My heavenly Father likes to hear *me* sing. I can't sing so sweetly as some. But my Father likes to hear me sing as well as those who sing better than I can. My Father likes to hear the crow as well as the nightingale, for He made them both."

CHAPTER FIFTEEN

BILLY LOVED children, and they loved him just as dearly. He never turned them away, and he so filled his sermons with lively and interesting stories that the children thronged to hear him. When at ease, he would take the little ones on his knee, bouncing them up and down to the joyous rhythm of some of his favorite hymns. One of the songs he especially loved was:

> "Come, let us rally round the cross,
>   Despising earthly Pleasure,
> And gladly reckon all things loss,
>   For Christ our heavenly treasure.
> Rejoice and sing, the Lord is King,
>   And we'll repeat the story,
> We'll make the heavenly arches ring
>   When we get home to glory."

One day Billy took some of his scarce money and went into the city of Truro to buy a new dress for his little girl. Of course she waited at home excited and eager to receive her frock, as little girls do. She kept running to the door, looking down the road to see if her father was coming with the new frock. Joey had given him a basket to carry it home in so that it would not get crushed as he carried it. But unsedate Billy Bray never fitted into a conservative, expected behavior mold. On the way home, thoughts of God's love surged into his heart. No doubt he heard one foot say "Glory" again, and the other echo "Hallelujah." At any rate, he must have leaped around very enthusiastically. Without realizing it, he danced the dress right out of the basket.

As he came into the house, his face wreathed in smiles, the little girl and Joey both asked him where the dress was that he had bought.

"Why, here it is!" But he stared at the empty basket almost stupidly. Billy's heart was filled with distress as he looked at Joey and his disappointed little daughter. But this did not cast his spirits down.

The next morning he went to a class meeting. One person stood and told about his troubles. Then another, long-faced and doleful, began to relate the trials he was suffering. Billy looked from one face to the other. "I've got trials, too," he said, "for yesterday I went into Truro and bought a frock for the little maid; coming home, I got to catching up my heels a little bit, and I danced the frock out of the basket."

Billy looked humble and careworn, in spite of his countenance glowing with faith in God. Those who had been expounding on their trials felt ashamed. They had so much more than the little Cornish preacher with the great faith.

They immediately collected enough money to give Billy to get his small girl another dress. And to Billy no journey had greater joy than when he went back to Truro with money from the "windows of heaven."

Two or three days afterward, the person who found the original dress returned it.

"I had two frocks for one. Glory!" Billy exclaimed. One day Billy and one of his more conservative friends trudged down the road to a missionary meeting. Suddenly Billy became silent, strange behavior for him. His friend glanced toward him and noted that his lips moved.

"What are you praying for, Billy?" asked the friend, his curiosity getting the better of him.

Billy turned, smiling, and informed his friend that he was praying for him. "I was just asking the Father to send down ten thousand-weight of glory on your soul."

The friend, telling of this singular experience afterward, said that for the first time in his life he felt almost compelled to praise God aloud. Billy was used to the feelings that his friend experienced for the first time.

"Come on, come on!" he cried, his face wreathed in smiles. "Come along, or we shall not be able to leave, for the lane is full of glory."

S. W. Christophers told of the time when he first met Billy. He, too, was charmed by the utter naivete of Billy's faith and trust in God. He delighted in the memory of his quaint sayings.

"If Billy gets work, he praises the Lord; when he gets none, he sings all the same. Billy once said, 'Do 'ee think He'll starve Billy? No, no, there's sure to be a bit of flour in the bottom of the barrel for Billy.' "

CHAPTER SIXTEEN

IT IS inconceivable that Billy Bray, a poor man with a large family, who had steady work in the mines, should do so much for God. His vision was tremendous. He had no horse to ride, only the open road—and feet certainly weary from long, arduous hours underground and tilling in his small garden to eke out his family's meager sustenance.

Other men with far more money, strength, and time lived in Cornwall at that time; but we do not know their names, though some of them called the little preacher silly, and harshly criticized his colorful aphorisms and enthusiastic antics.

Kerley Downs Chapel absorbed his interest and his faith after the completion of Bethel. He threw his whole soul into it, waiting upon the Lord in his own simple way. Of course promises of help flew about as usual, but in the end Billy had the burden of Kerley Downs Chapel mostly to himself.

The devil discouraged him when day after day Billy would come from the mine to discover himself the only one bearing the burden.

Naturally, in his weariness, his exuberance suffered. If they all had gone off and left, he thought, it would serve them right if he'd just go, too. Certainly he had enough to do around home and in his field and garden.

But Billy knew very well the source of such petulant thoughts. He believed firmly that if he resisted, the devil would flee; and that is just what he wanted him to do.

"Devil, doesn't thee know me better than that?" he demanded. "By the help of the Lord, I will have this chapel up, or lose my skin on the down."

As he hoped, the devil let him rest for a while, and he could work in peace with blistered hands and happy dreams of the many souls who would be born again in this structure. He dreamed of heaven and of the joy he would have when he met the souls he had been able to save.

When learned men came to his chapels and preached with a great show of rhetoric and oratory, Billy was sorely disappointed. Ever alert to the working of the Spirit of God, he would mutter, "He has a lot of *grammar*, but little of the *Father*." Billy's keen insight kept him from seeking the praises of men.

The first day he preached at Kerley Downs, two women, deeply touched, became converted. That first year, fifteen souls found Christ in the building his callous hands had erected. Billy praised the Lord for this because, to put it into his own words, "one soul is worth a thousand worlds!"

Word spread rapidly about Billy's activities in building the two chapels. One day, to his wonder and joy, a gentleman in the parish of Gwennap gave him a piece of land. He got right to work, and with a few neighbors to help, he soon had the foundation dug.

Billy's eager mind jumped ahead even while he was throwing out the earth, digging the foundation trench. Stone! That was needed next! A quarry near the railroad came to his mind. It had been worked so much that people thought there was little left. But Billy had observed a high place in the middle that no one had touched. To the quarry he went, amazing curious onlookers with the stone he got out of one hump in the middle. Complacent about all their objections, he informed them that he worked for a *strong* concern called the Father, Son, and Holy Ghost; such a company could never break.

Now Gwennap was a long way from his home. He had difficulties getting home, eating, and then walking the roundabout road to where the chapel was being built. It cut down on his working hours severely. But the Father in heaven took care of that. A gentleman nearby volunteered to give him five shillings a month for expense money—right when he needed it most.

This enabled Billy to eat at a little coffeehouse near the mine and go right on to Gwennap. It saved him a great deal of walking, for which he was humbly grateful.

Billy often called his source of supply for chapel building "the bank of heaven." When its balance began to get perilously low, the Lord always sent someone to build it up. He declared again and again that it was a strong bank, and he frequently withdrew the funds stored there by faith.

One evening as he was finishing his foundation, a Mr. T. came up to him. Billy was sure that the Lord had sent him, since the bank balance needed replenishing. "You'll want timber, and lime, and slate, will you not?" the man inquired.

Billy's delight knew no bounds. "Yes, sir; aye, and I do," he replied.

"Then go to my stores, Mr. Bray, and take out what you want."

It was like a blank check. Billy could see the walls rising already in his dreams, and he immediately engaged masons to do the work. While they were on the job, Billy walked for miles around the countryside asking people for money. He tackled farmers, fishermen, gentlemen, and an old miser never known to give a penny to anybody or anything. Billy got half a crown from the ragged old reprobate, who said he did not suppose he'd sleep well, having let that piece of money out of his hands.

Then he went on to St. Ives, a fishing village far to the north of Cornwall. His friend there, a Mr. Bryant, sighed and told him, "You've come to St. Ives at a bad time. Fishing has been poor, and the people are in great need of bread." Billy saw poverty and discouragement stalking everywhere in the small town.

But his mind went back as always to the glorious days when Jesus walked the earth. He spoke to Mr. Bryant about it. He told him that it must have been poor times back there on the Sea of Galilee, where the disciples fished all night and caught nothing. Maybe the Lord had sent him to St. Ives to urge the people to let down their nets on the *other* side of the ship.

The first thing Billy did was to call a meeting at the Wesleyan Chapel. When a large number of people came, Billy told them they must pray to the Lord to send in the fish. While they prayed, the fortune of the fishermen changed. And when they came out of the chapel, the poor women had great plates of pilchards to sell. To Billy's eyes, they fairly gleamed in the moonlight. The very air of the night and the attitude of the people changed completely.

The load of poverty lifted for many a poor family that night. Boats came into the harbor, drawn down almost to the waterline. And even the next day they hauled in more than eight thousand casks of fish. To the simple fisherfolk, this was a miracle such as had occurred only when Jesus walked the earth. By Monday the fishermen, jubilant at their turn of fortune, coaxed Billy to go out with them in their boats.

They not only promised him money for his chapel but fish to carry home to his family as well. From St. Ives, Billy carried away six pounds and fifteen shillings. Besides, a druggist gave him forty-two more shillings. Now Billy could pay the masons and the carpenters.

Every detail of Billy's spiritual career seems like a romance. It is a love story, for the Lord never had a more grateful and loving child than the humble little miner of Cornwall.

Even in finding a pulpit for Kerley Downs Chapel, Billy experienced the mighty providence of God. He did not ask for splendor, because the place he built was for Him who had "not where to lay his head." Yet he wanted good solid things that would last a hundred years.

He went over to a furniture auction in search of something from which be might devise a pulpit desk for the new place of worship. A curious old three-cornered cupboard, ancient, but strongly built, attracted his attention.

"The very thing!" cried the little preacher with delight. "The very thing. I can cut a slit down the back of it, and strengthen the middle of it, and put a board up in front of it, and clap a pair o' steers behind it, and then the preacher can preach out of it pretty."

Billy, not acquainted with the auction's rules, asked a man standing nearby what he thought that cupboard might sell for. The man told him it would probably bring six shillings. Then the man he questioned stared at Billy's face for a moment.

"Why, you're Billy Bray!" he exclaimed. Who would not recognize this man of God in that part of Cornwall? "Here," he added, I'll give 'ee the six shillings to buy it." Billy didn't bid right by starting low, as most people do.

In his eagerness to get a pulpit, he shouted that he would give six shillings as soon as the auctioneer put up the old antique for bids. To Billy's bewilderment and chagrin, another man outbid him and bought the cupboard.

People laughed at Billy's discomfiture and at his ignorance of auction procedure. Downcast, but not discouraged, Billy set out to hunt up the man who had given him the six shillings, but he had gone.

Still bewildered at the turn of affairs that he had been so sure was the work of the Lord, Billy set out on foot to his little chapel to ask the Lord about it. Inside its walls, which were answers to prayer, Billy felt anew the comfort and the blessing of God. His spirit was lifted, and he was sure all would be well.

Imagine his surprise after he left the chapel to see the cupboard he had needed going slowly up a hill nearby, loaded on a cart. Billy followed, filled with curiosity. The horse stopped in front of a cottage, and the man who had outbid Billy called a neighbor. They started to take it into the house.

But either the door had been made too small, or the cupboard was far too big. They turned it this way and that way, end for end, but could not get it in. The man who had bought it became more and more exasperated.

"I've given seven shillings for this," he exclaimed angrily; "now I shall have to break it up for firewood."

But Billy appeared at this moment. His blue eyes a-twinkle, he offered the man six shillings for the cupboard, provided he would deliver it to his chapel. Immediately the man accepted Billy's offer.

Even in this Billy saw the mercy of God. "Bless the Lord!" he rejoiced. "'This just like Him. He knew I couldn't carry it myself, so He got this man to carry it for me."

CHAPTER SEVENTEEN

IN ALL of Billy's Christian humility, he had a decided dignity and a very definite pride of heart. In England the "gentlemen," as the landed gentry and more opulent people were designated, received an exaggerated, groveling respect little understood by their American cousins.

Billy took a companion with him once on one of his many expeditions to raise funds. As they approached a vast manor house, the friend told Billy he thought it might be better if the two of them would go to the back door to present their requests. Billy looked indignant. "No!" he replied adamantly to the timorous suggestion. "No, I am the son of a King, and I shall go footways."

He did not fear the face of man, nor words, nor threats while on business for his heavenly King. The large estates owned vicious dogs to keep out peasants and trespassers. Often the estate owners hired watchmen, sharp of tongue and too ready with blows at times. But such did not deter the determined servant of the Lord.

Billy delighted in recounting stories of God's intervention. Hearing one particular story twice from the woman concerned, he told it many times, for it was his deepest pleasure to illustrate the power of God.

A woman named Florence Boskin had been so cruelly treated by a member of her family that she became a cripple. For seven years she did not have the use of one of her legs. She could not get about at all except by using a cane and a crutch. Moreover, her whole constitution was so impaired that, unable even to lift the one foot, she was obliged to drag it after her. There seemed no hope of her ever being able to walk again, for she had grown old.

The woman finally became totally bedridden. She lay there praying to the Lord, in whom she had all confidence since her conversion. That night the miracle occurred which Billy loved to relate. First God healed her soul of its bitterness and resentment toward people and life, which had dealt so harshly with her.

Light seemed to break through the gloom and blackness of her mind, and in place of sorrow, her soul filled with joy. The first step toward the kingdom had been taken. "Now, Lord," she cried out with joy, "You have healed my soul; why not heal my body, too?"

Out of the watches of the night, the still, small voice spoke to her. "Arise," came the message, "and go down to the Gospel-house, and there thou shalt be healed."

But she dreaded the night, the chill air, and the darkness so fearsome to a cripple. No street lamps lighted her way. Tremulously, she asked God why He could not heal her on her bed. Why need she take the painful, agonizing journey? As soon as she uttered this sentence, the feeling of glory left her.

Later it occurred to her why the Lord had asked this hard thing of her. It was so that many could be eyewitnesses to His power in healing her. Painfully she arose and dressed, then dragged her way down the stairs. Breakfast was hot and tempting. Surely she could stop and eat a bit before she started her wearisome trip.

But no! An urgent eagerness pushed her weary body on; no temptation could hold her back. She could do it! She could, indeed! And off she went, slowly dragging the helpless foot along the ground.

Her class leader, surprised to see her out so early and with such a look of glory on her plain face, saw her coming. "How is it you are down here so early today, Florence?" he asked.

"Great things are going to be done here today," she replied, gladness ringing in her voice. "I'm going to have a sound leg, for the Lord has told me so."

But the conservative class leader could not share her faith. He shook his head, not hesitating to tell her she was acting like a madwoman. "If you do not have a deal more faith than I have in this, you'll never be healed!" he declared.

But Florence did have more faith. With this blanket of discouragement thrown on her ardor, her faith actually seemed to grow rather than diminish. As the people prayed, she proclaimed, "Pray away, the balm is coming."

Then the miracle occurred, as surely as it had at the pool of Bethesda. The old woman threw away her crutch and stick and began to walk all over the chapel. People gasped with amazement. It hardly seemed possible. She walked without cane or crutch to the end of her life.

One time Billy took eighteen pence to buy medicine for his seriously ill child. On the way he met a man, desperate because of the hunger of his children. He had lost a cow and was out begging for money to get another so that his little ones could have milk. Billy just *had* to give that eighteen pence to the man to assist him in his need.

Returning home to Joey without money and without the medicine, he told her that the child would live. "The Lord has told me so," he declared. And Joey admitted that the little one had taken a turn for the better while he was gone.

Joey took ill herself one time. In her discouragement she complained to Billy that she couldn't see anything at all from heaven.

Billy's eyes must have twinkled and glowed at that. There beside his faithful Joey's bed, he began to recount miraculous happenings from the life of our Saviour. After each story he would say triumphantly, "If I *saw* it, I should not believe it more than I do now!"

Joey watched his expressive face as he recounted the glories of salvation. "So do *I* believe it, too!" she affirmed. Such was the home where God dwelt. Billy had seen great sorrow of heart, but now he dwelt in full joy.

He believed that the lowly—the underdog, the poor, and the despised—were doubly precious to the sympathetic Lord because of their lack of good things. Billy would walk for miles to render aid, to help someone in need, to carry food to the hungry or pray for the sick. Poor and needy himself, Billy always managed to find someone in worse poverty. He could not keep two of anything, but was bound, before a few hours elapsed, to find someone who had none.

But underneath it all was the real business part of the Christian life of Billy Bray; and that was to preach the gospel. It was like a harp of many strings that the gnarled, rough hand of Billy Bray continually played upon. Surely the music of his good works was sweet to the Father.

Billy was a trial to Joey sometimes. She was like Martha, troubled about many things, though she was a wondrously good woman. She bore patiently with him, never knowing exactly what her quaint husband might do. She knew many hardships from his free-heartedness and his inability to keep from helping those poorer than they. She would not have been human if she had not wished that sometimes she could count on the money from the mine. But the Lord always provided. If one thing didn't show up, something else did.

One day a minister had been called in to hold services in one of Billy's chapels. While there, he witnessed an incident that, but for him, would probably never have been known. One morning after the family had finished breakfast and family prayers, Billy went out. The minister was in his room studying when he heard a commotion at the door.

In came Billy carrying a tiny boy and a tiny girl, one on each arm, with their small arms twined about his neck. Joey looked up from her endless round of duties.

"Billy! Where are you going with those children?"

Then came the sorrowful tale that their mother had died, and the drunken father had run away and left them by the side of the stream. But Joey protested it was impossible to take on this added responsibility. They had a hard time feeding and clothing their own four. These little ones must go to the workhouse.

All workhouses in England were not as terrible as those described by Charles Dickens in *Oliver Twist*, but they were far from pleasant. The plight of the little children and the tragic look on their tear-stained faces wrung Billy's tender heart. The coldness, the rigid regime, and the unsympathetic routine of the usual workhouse would never be the lot of these little ones if Billy could help it.

"The Lord can as well feed them here as He can in the 'union,'" he declared, leading the two over to where his own little ones played.

"Here, my dears," he told them gently; "this is your home now."

Joey could not help feeling skeptical about this arrangement. Where the money would come from was more than she could fathom. This gave the visiting minister food for thought. He had a salary and no family, yet he knew that he would have hesitated about taking two children in for life with no more thought than that. Ashamed, he took his money out and counted it. He had just two pounds, fifteen shillings, and tenpence. Joey continued to be so distressed that he felt constrained to offer Billy some help with their keep.

"Here, Billy," he said; "here is five shillings toward the little orphans."

Billy's face lit up as he handed it to his wife, assuring her that the Lord had sent them five shillings before the children had even eaten a pennyworth.

Meanwhile, the listening minister felt embarrassed about his miserly offering in the face of Billy's gigantic generosity. He felt more like a thief than a benefactor. Before long he asked for the five back and laid ten shillings in Billy's hand.

Billy almost shouted at that. "Praise the Lord! Joey, didn't I tell you the Lord could feed them here as well as in the union?"

But the visiting minister did not feel much better at this exchange of the five for a ten. He did not feel the Lord's blessing. So he took back that half a sovereign and gave Billy a pound. By this time, Billy was in fine fettle. He began to shout and praise God, urging Joey to shout, too.

But the still, small voice kept urging until the minister put the entire two pounds and fifteen shillings in Billy's bands. When he wanted Billy to take the tenpence, he refused that. "No, brother," he said; "keep that to pay turnpike gates when you go home."

Billy offered a prayer of thanks so fervent that the whole room seemed vibrant with the glory of the Lord. Billy kept those children in his home until they were old enough to care for themselves.

Billy and Joey were lavish with the little they had. But their small income limited their ability to help. So with spiritual boldness, Billy went out to gather funds for the needy when he could.

At one wealthy home, the man donated money and the lady gave clothes. Then they invited Billy to tea in the lavish drawing room. The table was laid neatly with hot tea, sugar in a bowl, to be picked up with silver tongs, thin china cups, delicate little cakes, and bread and butter.

Billy's eyes glistened with tears at this unusual kindness from the rich man and his wife. And he did not leave until he had them all on their knees in prayer, the gentleman, his lady, servants, and all.

The kind of personal adornment Billy admired was the ornament of a meek and quiet spirit, though he embellished his own religion with more noise than some. When women adorned themselves lavishly and spent much money on flowers and artificials, Billy loudly condemned. To him all such vanities were silly and useless and detrimental to the welfare of the Christ-seeking soul. "I wouldn't mind you having a wagonload of them on your heads, if that would do you any good; but you know it wouldn't, and all persons know that flowers only grow in soft places."

Men felt his barbs, too, when he saw them conceited, dressed like dandies, and wasting good money on useless fripperies. If they waxed their moustaches, he reprimanded them for "oiling their cobs," or "twirling their whiskers, spending more time at these vain things than they spent in prayer and reading the Bible.

He felt that people who followed after the fashions of the day were working hard to destroy the fence which should separate the church from the world.

People prone to put off breaking their evil habits until a more convenient day, Billy warned, "It is dangerous to put off our soul's salvation until we are on our deathbed; for where there is one who gets the prize, there are ten who lose it, and the same old devil that got at them downstairs will get at them when they are in their beds."

Billy knew people so poor, neglected, and needy that it seemed as if the whole world had forgotten and forsaken them. One such old woman had a crippled daughter. They lived in one squalid, miserable room. It was dirty and ill-kept, for with deep poverty often comes carelessness and discouragement.

Billy's bright eyes took in the squalor and wretchedness, the rags and tatters, and the almost bare cupboard. His blue eyes dimmed with sympathy. Hardly a detail of the meanness and misery escaped him.

The old woman began to recount to the little minister her troubles and trials, and they were many. She told of a fierce storm that tore the roof from her little abode.

"Heaven will be a 'pretty' place for you when you get there, Billy comforted her in his kindest tone. "You will be able to say, 'What a glorious place I am in now! I am not now down in the house with the roof blown away; I am not now in a dirty little room, with little meat and clothes—oh, what a mighty change is this! What a glorious place is heaven!'"

Another time Billy chided a wife for mourning terribly about her husband's approaching death. He launched into such a vivid and glorious portrayal of the saints' inheritance that the wife began to smile and wipe away her tears.

He pictured the honor it would be if Queen Victoria should call her husband to come to London to see her and live in a palace, surrounded with fantastic riches. Then he contrasted this with the glories that the Saviour has laid up for those who choose to love and obey Him. In contrast to what the Lord has prepared and what the Saviour is, the queen is only mortal. She may die, and all would be lost. Not so with Jesus, he explained.

Billy declared triumphantly, "The Lord Jesus Christ is at all the expense of the 'fit-out'; He provides the robe in which your husband will be clothed, the crown that he will wear, the palm that he will wave."

He made heaven so real, the presence of the Lord so gracious and inviting, that the sickroom seemed vibrant with the holy presence. Billy had that gift, a gift from the Lord.

One day Billy's supervisor instructed him to work in the mines, but Billy felt it his duty to attend church at Hicks Mill Chapel. One of the levels of the mine in which he worked filled with water every twelve hours and needed to be pumped out. When Billy had to leave, he felt confident that the Lord would take care of this duty for him.

Nonetheless, he faced trouble when he went back to work the next morning. He went early—at six o'clock—for he felt that the water was his responsibility that day, since the Lord took care of it the day before so that he could go to church.

But the boss, whom he called the "captain," was highly indignant over his behavior. He asked him angrily why he had not come to work.

"It was not the Lord's will that I come," came the humble but decisive reply.

"I'll 'Lord's will' thee!" shouted the angry man. "Thou shalt not work here any more." This was a serious threat, for Billy needed the work to support his growing family.

Even then the poor stipend he received was far from adequate. But he did not show the least excitement or dismay.

In the end, the mine rehired Billy, and things were even better for him than before. He had more freedom to attend meetings after he calmly stood for the right.

Fired from one job, he turned around and found another at more than double the pay. Billy's faith in God was continually rewarded. He firmly believed in the God who promised, "Them that honour me I will honour."

One day he felt impressed to fast. That day he had more success winning souls than he had had for many years. He therefore made it a rule to fast one day a week.

One of his neighbors, Richard Verran, feared for Billy's health and spoke to him about his fasting. "The devil is trying to starve thee," he told Billy kindly, "for he knows what great things the Lord has done for thee."

But Billy, convinced about fasting, replied swiftly and assuredly. "Richard," he said, smiling, "the devil shall not starve me, for I can soon know by asking the Lord, who will tell me whether I am right or no."

He knelt and addressed the Lord as assuredly as he would a friend: "Lord, Thou knowest what the people are saying, that I shall starve myself if I fast; now, my dear Lord, if I must not fast, make me happier than I have been."

But the expected thrill of happiness did not surge through Billy just then. Again he asked, "Lord, must I fast?"

The power of God came upon Billy with such force that he fell off his kneeling stool, convincing him more than ever that he should fast.

Of his fast day, he always said that he got his breakfast and his dinner at the King's table, and he declared that he would not exchange these spiritual meals for anything.

Billy Bray

Billy Bray's Three Eyes Chapel

CHAPTER EIGHTEEN

WHILE BILLY was busy preaching the Christian gospel, strange new things were happening in the world. Peter Cooper had built Tom Thumb, the first successful railroad locomotive to be used in the United States. William Miller, in America, and Edward Irving, in England, had begun to preach the second coming of the Lord. Queen Victoria became the bride of her beloved Prince Albert; and Alexander Graham Bell was a tiny baby up in Edinburgh, Scotland.

The stirrings of a restless world found few echoes in Cornwall, however. The people were poor, and few were able to get newspapers. Although Livingstone had started his amazing work in Africa, it is not likely that Billy ever heard of him. He was too busy working in the mine, helping the needy, visiting the sick, building chapels, praying, and praising his Lord.

How was *he* to know that 1840 saw the "penny black" issued, the first postage stamp in Victorian England? He did not get letters, nor did he write them, but he knew one thing that few Christians ever learn in a lifetime of struggle. He learned to rejoice and be glad, even in time of persecution, temptation, and hardship.

It seems strange, so complete was his conversion, that Billy should be tempted to do evil, to swear, even to lie. But the devil attacked him continuously. More than once, his trials great, his miseries sore, he felt tempted to end it all, to commit suicide by throwing himself down the shaft of the mine. But the wiry little miner-preacher caught himself with a jerk when that frightful way of ending his worries occurred to him.

"Do it yourself, Old Smutty Face," he retorted to the devil. "Do it, an' see how *you* like it."

Billy's conversations with the devil were as real to him as if he were talking to a fellow worker in the mines. And he had retorts that he hoped would settle the "old boy."

Devil: I'll have thee down to hell after all.

Billy: Hast thee got a little "lew" [sheltered] place for me in hell where I could sing thee a song? Thee couldn't burn me, Devil. There's no grease in me. What an old fool thee art now. I have been battling with thee for twenty-eight years, and I have always beat thee, and I always shall.

Devil: Well, I'll have thee down to hell after all.

Billy: I'd as soon go to hell with thee as not. For I'd bring Jesus Christ with me, and shout and sing, and praise the Lord, for that's a sound thee hasn't heard for two seven years.

Devil: Thou art a fool to go and preach.

Billy: Not so big a fool as thee art, for once thee was in a good situation, and did not know how to keep it.

Billy lived in a superstitious era, when ghosts and spirits and hobgoblins were the common belief of most people. Billy had not been converted so long that all of these superstitions and fears had left him.

Naturally, Billy had seen death in the mines. Often the rickety wooden supports would collapse and dump tons of rock on friends he had gone down into the mine with only a few hours before. Place after place in the dark shafts and tortuous tunnels had been scenes of such tragedies. In the dense darkness, only feebly lit by the small hat lamps, Billy's fears could be easily aroused. Ideas of hell and of the devil, entirely out of step with Bible teaching, came easily to mind.

At one place in the dark shaft he had to cross a bridge. So nervous was he that he almost thought the old devil would meet him in the middle of the bridge. But his ever-present faith came to his rescue, even as the Bible promised: "[He] will not suffer you to be tempted above that ye are able; but will with the temptation also make a way to escape, that ye may be able to bear it."

Billy shouted aloud in the darkness, "The devil! Who is he? What can he do? The devil is a fallen angel! He was turned out of heaven by God! He is held now in chains! I am Billy Bray!

God is my heavenly Father! Why should I fear the devil?"

His courage and faith grew stronger every second in the dense, heavy blackness. He continued to shout his defiance to his ever-present foe:

"Come on, then, thou devil; I fear thee not! Come on, old ones and young ones, black ones and blue ones, fiery and red-hot ones; come on, Devil, and all thy ugly hosts!"

His heart at ease, the miner-preacher plodded on his way. Soon his delight mounted, and he began to sing and dance because of his spiritual victory.

Joey, although a good woman, was not above loudly chiding her humble husband for the hard straits in which they often found themselves. Her accusation that he was the cause of their poverty and privation was too near the truth for him to venture a reply.

Yet though the wolf snarled near, even scratched their door, it did not get in. At one time, as Joey had exhausted her impatience on Billy's head, a friend came to the door with a large basket of provisions.

Believing strongly that the Lord would not let them starve, Billy sang about it in his peculiar thin voice:

"Not fearing or doubting,
With Christ on my side,

I hope to die shouting,
The Lord will provide."

He often took his wages to pay for some item needed in the chapels he continued to build. His wife constantly told him they would all end up in the poorhouse.

"Never mind, my dear Joey, the Lord will provide," he would assure her, his eyes gleaming with confidence. Again and again he found his faith tried to the breaking point, but God never failed him.

One story of providence Billy loved to relate. Here is how he tells it:

"At one time I had been at work the whole of the month but had no wages to take up when payday came; and as we had no bread in the house, Joey advised me to go up and ask the captain [boss] to lend me a few shillings, which I did. He let me have ten shillings. On my way home I called to see a family, and found they were worse off than myself; for though we had no bread, we had bacon and potatoes, but they had neither.

"So I gave them five shillings, and went towards home. Then I called on another family, and found them, if possible, in greater distress than the former. I thought I could not give them less than I had given the others; so I gave them the other five shillings, and went home."

We can well imagine with what misgivings he approached home. He knew Joey would be outraged, and well she might be. He entered quietly, laid his old hat down, and looked at her humbly.

"Well, William, have you seen the captain?"

"Yes. "

"Did you ask him for any money?"

"Yes; he let me have the ten shillings."

"Where is it?"

"I have given it away."

"I never saw such a fellow as you in my life. You are enough to try anyone."

"The Lord isn't going to stay in my debt very long," Billy answered quietly, and he took his hat and left the house.

Joey, discouraged and downhearted for several days after that, found it hard to eat without bread, even though they had meat and potatoes. Billy endured her downcast face in humble silence. He came and went from work, listened to the complaining, and ate his frugal meals in silence. Then one afternoon when he came home from the mine, the whole atmosphere seemed changed. Joey was cheerful, even gay. Billy knew something good had happened, but he waited for her to tell him.

"Mrs. —— has been here today," she said.

"Oh!"

"And she gave me a sovereign."

Billy's old exuberance returned. He smiled broadly. "There, I told you the Lord wasn't going to stay in my debt very long; there's the ten shillings, and ten shillings interest."

Again and again he appealed to the Father for help in even the small things that disturbed his peace. When his shoe sole, worn and rotten, fell off in the deep mud, he called the Father's attention to the fact that those shoes had been worn out in His service.

Only a few days later, a friend asked Billy to go with him to the city of Truro. In his ragged flapping shoes, Billy went. Not only did the kind friend outfit Billy with new shoes, but with clothing as well.

Again and again someone supplied Billy with clothing right when he needed it. When he first became a Christian, he had only a ragged jacket, but since he had no better, he wore it to the meeting. He did not wear it long. A kind Quaker gentleman gave him a strong jacket which lasted a long time.

A man told him once that the Lord had told him to give Billy some clothing he had there. "But I do not know whether they will fit you," he added, ruefully.

Billy's face lit up with gladness, as always, at an unexpected providence. "If the good Lord told you to do it, they will fit me!" he cried.

Billy bore all his trials by taking them to the Lord, and the blessings he received far outweighed his sorrow. Even the anguish of losing his Joey after a long illness did not dampen his faith. He was impressed by the Holy Spirit that his wife and his whole family would be saved. Even losing his love, his darling wife, didn't obscure the promises. He was sure he would be with Joey again. "She is mine forever" so impressed his grieving mind that he burst into tears of joy.

CHAPTER NINETEEN

BILLY wanted to be fair to everyone. He knew he could not pretend to be a follower of Christ and at the same time be shady in his dealings, seeking the best for himself.

At one time a mine employed him in the capacity of captain-dresser. He had charge of processing a quantity of ore, his profits to be derived from the metal taken. The job worried him, for a number of young people had been assigned to work under him. If the ore proved to be worthless, then all their hard, grueling labor would be for nothing. Neither would Billy, with his growing family, get any pay.

The thing that troubled him most was not his own probable loss of time and money. He feared that the work of the Lord would suffer and fall into disrepute if such a thing occurred.

"Why, the people will say," he thought, "'There's that old Billy Bray, an old Bryanite, an old rogue. He hath cheated the boys and maidens of their wages. A pretty Christian, he!'"

Billy considered this a matter of prayer, so he got down on his skinny knees and talked to the Lord about the matter. Just as if the Lord didn't know a thing that was going on, Billy reviewed all the ramifications, telling him how many people would be hurt, inconvenienced, and go hungry if it proved to be a worthless pile of ore.

After much prayer, God gave Billy the assurance that He was "on His way." "I will bring thee through," came the small voice.

People's opinions might have discouraged Billy, had he not wholeheartedly taken the Lord at His word. Once he had that assurance, his sights ahead cleared. No matter how disparagingly anyone spoke, he would say stoutly, "I don't care whether the stuff is worth anything or not. The Lord hath told me He will bring me through, and I believe Him."

All doleful predictions proved false, to Billy's delight. On the day when they sampled the ore, it proved to be more valuable than anyone had dreamed. Everyone was well paid, and even Billy got five pounds for his share.

Since no place in Cornwall is far from the sea, Billy became well acquainted with the language of the fishing crews and with the nautical jargon of the sea. He would become greatly aggravated over the continual interference of the devil. He'd think in his naive and eccentric mind of different ways he'd like to trap the devil. No inquisitor of the Dark Ages had a bigger imagination for novel punishments than did Billy.

On the vessels coming into Falmouth Bay or St. Ives, Billy often observed the spool-shaped capstan, which the seamen turned by means of levers, winding a rope around it to raise the anchor.

He conceived a delightful idea of how lovely it would be to get the devil entangled hopelessly in the strong, taut ropes of the capstan. It afforded him great amusement to even contemplate it.

"The best way to serve the devil," declared Billy Bray, "is to wind him up at the capstan. Throw the rope around him, and turn away until you get him up close to the axle, and when he cries, 'Strike!' you mustn't let go at all, but hold fast. If you get him up tight to the axle, and keep him there, he'll never be able to harm thee; he'll only be able to grizzle at thee."

Boys used to try to play pranks on the enthusiastic preacher. They would gather on dark nights, hide, and make weird noises, counting on superstition to scare the little man into fits. But Billy had long ago overcome such fear. He had been scolded, laughed at, jeered at, and treated with scorn.

One night a formidable group got together and made an unearthly hullabaloo behind a thick hedge. To the disappointment of the big boys, he seemed hardly aware of the noise. One young man, bolder than the rest, called loudly, "I'm the devil up here in the hedge, Billy Bray." Unperturbed, Billy marched on. "Bless the Lord! bless the Lord!" he cried with joy. "I did not know thee wost so far away as that!"

Billy loved to go to Truro. It presented a beautiful picture, with its spacious streets and sturdy granite buildings. Through the principal street flowed Truro Creek, deep enough to accommodate vessels of seventy tons—sizable ships then—right up to the town quay. Truro was one of the ancient tin coinage towns. It was a metropolis which the people visited with pleasure.

One time Billy stayed at a friend's house in the old city. At family prayers the mistress of the household read the account from the fourth chapter of Matthew about the temptation of our Lord. Billy followed the narrative of His fasting, and of the tempter coming to Him. He acted as if he had never read it before, though he had, many times.

His interest grew greater as the poignancy of the temptation increased. At last, when she read, " 'The devil taketh him up into an exceeding high mountain, and sheweth him all the kingdoms of the world, and the glory of them,' " Billy's excitement grew to fever pitch. The woman read on: " 'And saith unto him, All these things will I give thee, if thou wilt fall down and worship me.'"

Billy leaped to his feet and shouted, "The old vagabond! The old vagabond! How could he give away all the kingdoms of the world when he never had an old 'tatur skin to call his own, the old vagabond!"

Billy had many battles to wage, for in some things he himself had been enslaved. He knew how galling bonds could be. He had maintained for a while the soothing attitude toward strong drink of "Know how to carry your liquor. Know when to stop. A little drop will do you good, warm you when you're cold, pep you up when you're tired, and make the world seem a gayer, happier place."

Deep inside Billy knew that these excuses were from the devil.

Billy had been a slave to both liquor and tobacco. He knew all too well the urgency, the agony, the nervousness, that came when these habits were not gratified, so he was loath at first to even go to a temperance meeting when a Mr. Teare was to lecture. He certainly did not intend to sign any pledge, for "a little drop, if a man does not take too much, will do him good," he had always thought.

But Billy had built up no permanent walls of prejudice. When he became Christ's child, his heart opened to additional knowledge. The more he listened, the more searching became the relentless light of truth. Intemperance in all its cruelty and ugliness was revealed. Right while Mr. Teare was in the middle of his lecture, Billy could stand it no longer.

A friend of his, Thomas Tregaskis, sat a little nearer to the speaker than he did. Uninhibited, Billy spotted him near the speaker's table. "Thomas! Thomas!" he shouted. The speaker stopped in amazement, but Billy paid him no heed, so intent was he to get the deed done. "Put down my name! Put down my name!"

The commotion caused a laugh, but it offered proof of the convincing quality of the lecture.

No one knew more than Billy how low he had fallen in his youth. Now it was as plain as letters of fire that a child of Christ can't indulge in strong drink or tobacco.

British towns all have their pubs, as public houses were called. Billy called his chapels "heaven houses." He did not have such a complimentary name for the pubs. He knew of one "hell house" where nineteen men had at various times gotten drunk and gone to work in the mine, only to fall to their death down a shaft.

He saw the filthiness of tobacco, too, though as yet its evils had not been proved in the crucible of science. He declared once that he loved tobacco so much that he would rather have his pipe than his dinner, if he had to take a choice.

He finally quit because he realized that the only acceptable service, the only acceptable worship, came from one with clean hands and clean lips. But it took a woman to convince Billy to make the final break with the habit.

Mary Hawke came to visit him, and while she was there, he took out his pipe, filled it with tobacco, and started to smoke. She looked at him a moment.

"Do you not feel it is wrong to smoke?" she asked. The question pierced him like a thorn. He took his pipe out of his mouth.

"Something inside me has told me it is an idol, and a lust," he replied cautiously.

"That was of the Lord," observed his guest.

Billy got up, threw his tobacco into the fire, and broke the pipe under his feet.

"Now I *must* give it up," he decided. "The Lord is telling me of it inside, and now this woman comes and tells me outside. So the tobacco must go, love it as I may."

It was a hard chore, for every cell of his body seemed to cry out for it when he stopped so suddenly. Billy never did go back to it, though he suffered so intensely that he had to plead for the Lord's help.

He had a severe test the very next day, to add to the gnawing longing for tobacco. He was seized with an agonizing toothache which *seemed* to be caused from discarding tobacco. But Billy, determined to quit smoking, exclaimed, "I'll not smoke again even if I lose every tooth in my head!"

Then he resorted again to the Lord. He reminded Him of His words, "My yoke is easy, and my burden is light." When he had said that, the Lord honored his prayer and the pain left.

Billy made the error of trying to soothe his agonies from quitting smoking by chewing a little. But the "clean lips" thought burned into him like a coal of fire, and he finally conquered that as well, after a fearful struggle.

He was hard on preachers who continued both habits. He had little use for their loud professions and prayers.

One day Billy was asked to pray in a meeting held by one such minister.

"O Lord," he prayed, "help the people to give up their idols." "Amen!" cried the preacher. "Help Thy people to give up their ribbons and feathers." "Amen!" shouted the preacher again. "And their cups and drinks."

A little weaker "Amen" this time.

"And their pipes and tobacco!"

No response.

Billy opened his eyes. "Where's your 'Amen,' brother?" demanded Billy. "Why don't you say 'Amen' to the pipes as well as the cups. Ah! you won't say 'Amen' to the pipes!"

He went on with the prayer. But the preacher, angry with Billy, took him to task afterward!

Billy asked him pointedly why he could be so enthusiastic about other people giving up their idols when not willing to relinquish his. It did not seem consistent.

The minister had no answer.

CHAPTER TWENTY

BILLY BRAY could not see sin, quarreling, drunkenness, immorality, and frivolity without doing something about it. His success with people lay in his eccentricity and naïveté. He would use entreaties and loving arguments until the sinner in remorse forgot his anger. He enjoyed anyone and everyone, and he always said a word about Christ.

He never let an opportunity to help someone go by. He seemed to know just how to soften the hearts of the angry, and he had an inner perception about when to talk and when to keep silent.

While working one day on one of his many chapels, word came regarding a saintly brother who had, under great provocation, done a grave wrong. His wife, godless and wicked, railed against her husband, humiliated him, and tormented and persecuted him. She infested his Christian path with many thorns. She seemed bound to cause her husband to sin.

One day she actually threw a bucket of water in his face. Then he did explode, and he cursed her angrily. People heard him, of course; and his wife was actually glad she had caused her meek, long-suffering husband to lose his temper.

Tormenting him constantly, she published his one error far and wide. Discouraged, the man could hardly lift his head, Her loud accusations all seemed true. Now with his influence ruined, no one would look on him as a true Christian anymore, he feared. Then Billy Bray appeared to help this brother "overtaken in a fault."

Immediately the wretch of a wife appeared, a self-righteous smirk on her cruel face. She began to tell Billy in a loud voice just how wicked and mean her husband really was. Billy, swift to detect the note of triumph in her hateful voice, turned and looked right through her with piercing blue eyes.

"'He that is without sin among you, let him first cast a stone,'" Billy quoted to her distinctly. Then he took hold of the grieving, broken man and led him away. Heaven-born grace seemed to crown Billy's head that day. Comforting verses of the Bible poured from his lips. The man looked at him wonderingly. How could this wise little man find out that he thought it now no use to pray? How could he know that he thought no one would believe in him anymore?

Slowly Billy helped the man regain confidence in Christ, helped him escape his depression.

His wife, however, never ceased to harden her heart. She made life as hard as she possibly could for her husband. But God sometimes says, "Thus far shalt thou go and no farther." Death suddenly removed her.

A wealthy old man felt—perhaps rightly—that Billy's sermons and reproofs were too pointed. Because they too often concerned his practices and habits, he became one of Billy's most hateful persecutors. Instead of using his means, his life, and his will to forward the work of God, he exhausted his hatred on the head of the Cornish preacher.

Billy was probably aware of his attitude and saddened by it, but not often, for he was too busy.

Then life struck back at the old man. Lying stricken with illness in the richness of his beautifully appointed house, he could find no peace. He had no light for the path on which he stumbled now. Pride is humbled at such an hour, and the old reprobate sent for the man on whom he had wasted so much energy in hatred.

Billy came, but as he entered the broad hall and glimpsed great rooms resplendent with fine carpets, shining furniture, and rich hangings, he began in his quaint way to talk about the poverty of Christ when He lived on earth. He talked as if to himself, wondering quietly whether Jesus, on His mission of mercy to this world, ever occupied a place so opulent, so magnificently appointed. Did He, who got even His tribute money by a miracle, expend His means to gratify contemporary fashion?

The silent household listened with rising indignation as he elaborated on the grueling poverty of the Lord from His humble Nazareth home to the days of His ministry. In death His body was anointed with spices brought by friends, and wrapped in a donated winding sheet and placed in a borrowed tomb.

Billy, in his gentle way, had ruthlessly touched a sore spot. He knelt down then by the great bed, heavily draped and curtained with tapestry, folded his work-worn hands, and addressed his Friend above.

Looking at Billy's face, half smiling from inner joy, vibrating with sweet communion, his hearers were bound to find peace. The drawn, anxious lines on the old man's face relaxed. His troubled heart had begun to receive spiritual balm. The family and the man himself begged Billy to stay on until he should pass away.

How strange for Billy, living in a thatch-roofed miner's hut, to be an honored guest in a rich man's home! How strange to eat the finest of foods prepared by servants' hands!

Billy's weeks there were hectic, for the devil does not release his hold easily. Lips used to harsh words had to learn softness. Thoughts long running down grooves of hate had to be rearranged.

Victory finally came. Happy beyond words, Billy left the mansion, eager to see the little house he loved and the old furniture, familiar and restful.

By this time the Civil War had ended in America, and Bismarck had begun his blood, iron, and fire maneuvers to unite Germany.

Henry Ford toddled as a small child in Michigan, and the Atlantic cable had just been laid.

Down at Plymouth, Billy helped the Primitive Methodists with some meetings. He also lent his aid to a series in Devonport.

The way Billy praised the Lord irritated a few conservative people. One man took him to task for this on the street one day.

Billy answered sharply, for he had been reproved for this exuberance of spirit too often. "My best friend is the dear Lord," he cried. "He has made me *glad*, and no one can make me *sad*; He makes me *shout*, and there is no one who can make me *doubt*; He it is that makes me *dance and leap*, and there is no one that can keep down my *feet*."

Billy continued humble, tireless, ever on the lookout for good he could do. When he reached his seventy-fourth year, he alluded to his age as his fourth year of childhood. "You must excuse all faults and blunders," he said simply. "You do not expect so much from a child as from a man, and I am now in my fourth year of childhood, and therefore I may be a little simple and weak."

He did not cease his labors for his beloved Lord. He took long journeys, visiting with the poor, sick, and sad. He was always happy, full of confidence and bright faith. Even as age crept upon him, the irresistible urge kept the old legs on the move. His spiritual zeal never flagged.

In his ledger, where he made notes of his coming and going, he wrote on February 10, 1868, "In the morning after I had breakfast, bad as I was, I thought I would go to see some friends; and after calling on some of them, I went home. But I had hard work to get home, I was so ill; and my breath was short."

At one of the last meetings he was able to attend, even though his body was feeble, weak, and infirm, he wrote, "We could do nothing but praise, for the Spirit was poured out in such a wonderful manner. I was as happy as I could be and live. It was one stream of glory."

When he left the meeting, he could hardly make it home. He asked for the truth from the doctor when he sent for him. When told that he was going to die, Billy Bray shouted for joy. When someone asked him if he feared death, his face took on a look of glory.

"What! me fear death?...Why, my Saviour conquered death." His last word was, "Glory!" as he passed to his rest on Monday, May 25, 1868.

Buried at Baldhu church, Billy there awaits the resurrection of the just.

Jesus was real to Billy Bray, and heaven a place to be yearned after, because he knew he was a son of God. Billy will know Jesus when He comes because he knew Him so well on earth.

**Billy Bray's grave by the south wall
of Church of St. Michael at Baldhu**

Billy Bray's grave